THE FORTY YEAR OLD
ROOKIE

C. G. LAMBERT

Also by C. G. Lambert

Uncle Reggie Stories (Geek Lit)

The Kids Who Lived In A Hole

The Man In The Hotel Ceiling

The Girl From Wonderland

Standalones

You Had Me at Ice Cream (RomCom)

The Illiterate Prince (Fantasy)

Non-Fiction

Adventures in Analytics

This is a work of fiction. Names, characters, places, and incidents either are the product of the author's imagination or are used fictitiously. Any resemblance to actual persons, living or dead, events, or locales is entirely coincidental.

Copyright © 2025 by C.G. Lambert

All rights reserved. No part of this book may be reproduced or used in any manner without written permission of the copyright The Moral Right of the author is asserted.

First paperback edition August 2025

Typeset in Varsity and Palatino Linotype

Cover Art by Angela Pearse

ISBN 978-1-914531-05-7 Paperback (KDP)

ISBN 978-1-914531-06-4 Paperback (IngramSpark)

ISBN 978-1-914531-07-1 ePUB (IngramSpark)

www.cglambert.com

www.clamp.pub

To all beer league players, especially the Orcas and the Tigers.

The Bar

No adventure worth telling begins with a salad for dinner and an early night. You have to be open to the universe and jump when the opportunity presents itself. I didn't realize quite what the future had in store for me when my flatmate Seb called me late in the afternoon one Tuesday in June.

"Are you still looking for work?" he asked.

"Sure, have you got something?" I responded. I was a little puzzled because he was a journalist and I was in software. Maybe he had a lead on some work for me?

"Not really but if you fancy a jolly, I've got two slots on a visit to the Army Research Laboratory in Maryland. My photographer pulled out so if you pay the name change fee on the airline tickets, you're in."

"Wow, sounds good. When is it?"

"Our flight is at 9pm tonight which gives us just enough time to get to the airport and have a few beers while we wait for the plane. Meet you there at 6."

"Hey, I don't have any gear or anything. Won't they know I'm not a real photographer?"

"Have you got an iPhone?"

"Sure."

"Just wander around energetically and mutter things about the light being better at this angle and no one will doubt you."

"Okay… if you say so." I wasn't convinced, but just like that, we were off. Seb was a force of nature and typically bent reality to his way of thinking.

There were no hiccups at the ticket desk, a minimal fee to change the name and then I was on to security. The TSA agent with the wand gave me a double take when I came through. I cut a pretty noteworthy figure I guess. I was tall, three inches shy of two meters or six foot four in freedom measurement, and I had a 'Dad bod'. A keg instead of a six-pack, and a pretty impressive beard, more salt than pepper, that came down to my chest. I also had a shaven head because of a receding hairline. If I wore a plaid shirt and bib overalls, I would fit into any redneck bar, but my personal style was a little more bland with a pair of jeans, a t-shirt and a windbreaker. Mr. TSA waved me through when he caught a glimpse of a guy in a turban three spots behind me, and so I gratefully made my way to the bar. Seb was waiting there, a beer in front of my chair and his already half empty. He was average height and my age, so forty, and those years of drink hadn't been kind. He had a smaller paunch than mine, and his hairline was more intact, but a smattering of broken veins across his cheeks gave him the rosy glow of a few drinks, even when he was sober. He was English, with a posh accent at odds with his rough around the edges look.

"Catch up!" he said, raising a hand in greeting.

"Steady on! What's the rush?"

"My employer is paying for this, so I want to make sure we get the most out of it."

Ahh, that made sense. Tomorrow was going to be interesting. At this age, I had fallen out of the habit of operating with a hangover, so I wondered if I should switch to the lower alcohol beer.

The bar was across the concourse from our gate so there was little chance that we would miss our flight. But there was a chance, so I made a concerted effort to memorize the flight number and keep a beady eye on the departures board.

We made short work of the first beer and Seb handed me his company credit card. "Your turn," he said, gesturing towards the bar.

This arm of the terminal was surprisingly quiet and so there were only a few other patrons; one guy looking morose near our table and a pair of business travelers in the other corner. I walked up to the bartender.

"We might be here a while and if you could make sure I always get the low strength beer, that would be appreciated." He nodded in understanding. I pulled out my wallet and slipped him a ten. "And if you hear anyone being paged, can you give us a nudge just in case we don't hear it?"

He smiled and pocketed the note. I took the two drinks back to our table, making sure Seb got the full strength one. "So tell me about this Advanced Warfare base."

Seb took a sip before responding. "It's where the army shows off their latest and greatest technology, mainly to politicians so they can increase spending, and also to the real press, but sometimes we get an invite too. The Army must be trying to rustle up some more funding because one, they're inviting our magazine and two, they're paying for flights, an overnight hotel and all transfers. It's like a package holiday."

"Except instead of a beach resort in Tijuana, we're getting to watch Cyber Rambo in Maryland."

"It'll be fun! The Army won't blink when they reimburse the magazine, so we can cut a little loose. Even if you don't get any good photos, the press office will make sure we're covered with some photos from their press kit. Bargain!"

"Too good to be true!"

"Excuse me, are you heading to the Advanced Warfare base in Maryland?"

We turned and the morose man had scooted across two seats so he was adjacent to us. He had a slight build with a haunted expression like a dog who had been kicked too many times.

I shot Seb a look like 'Who is this guy?' but Seb was naturally gregarious and kicked into social mode, smiling broadly. "We certainly are! Do you know it?"

Mr. Morose stared through Seb, momentarily focusing on the distance two feet behind him. "It's funny, those companies that build those military gadgets, don't you think? For every Boston Dynamics that shows the training progress of their robots, there are a hundred other companies operating under the radar."

I adjusted my seat to face our new friend. "But surely if they're producing things for the military, then at least the Army, the generals and Congress get progress updates?"

"Ah yes," said our new friend. "But what about the ones that aren't producing for the military? Or...," he said, looking around the bar conspiratorially. "What about the ones who aren't producing for *our* military?"

Seb frowned. "What do you mean? Someone in Northrop-Grumman or General Dynamics is in fact making jets for the Chinese? Seems a little far-fetched, don't you think?"

Mr. Morose leaned back in his seat, shaking his head. "No, I don't think you're getting my point at all," he said. I could almost see the cogs in his head whirling as he changed tack. "So, you know that a lot of people reported UFOs back in the day – I'm talking the fifties and sixties. There was a concerted effort to paint those reporting sightings as nutcases and delusional psychos, and then the number of reports dropped off and there was a lull. Fast forward to the age of the iPhone, and with video and photographic evidence, we're back to a similar level of UFO sightings. Oh, sorry, we call them UAPs now, don't we? But now the influx of reports are from people of repute – pilots, that sort of thing. Now that every person with an iPhone is a citizen reporter, there is more evidence of them."

"Aliens," Seb nodded, trying to ingratiate himself.

A flash of anger crossed Mr. Morose's face. "No, not aliens. Why is everything that's unknown explained by them being aliens? So, a whole bunch of those recent sightings are explained away by weather balloons or by lens flare but there are a whole bunch which aren't explained. But they don't have to be aliens."

"There was one recently off the coast of Los Angeles, near the Navy's testing site," offered Seb.

"Right! What better place to test inventions than a place where other people are already testing their inventions?"

"What? You're saying that some R&D company is testing their machines in the Navy testing area?"

"With, or perhaps without, the Navy's knowledge."

"But those machines - Phil, you remember those, right?"

"Yeah, they were tic-tac shaped machines that ignored the rules of physics. Well, some of them anyway. They showed up on radar but didn't have any source of propulsion and did maneuvers which were impossible because they would have been pulling 20Gs."

"That's funny, because when you think about it, one of the reasons you would not want control surfaces or propulsion would

7

be if you were going to do things like pull 20 Gs, right?" Mr. Morose looked like he had just dropped a truth bomb which should have blown our minds but me and Seb just stared at him blankly. He rolled his eyes. "If you go like this...," He made a hand gesture of a very quick 90-degree turn. "If you wanted to do that at speed and high up in the air and you had wings, and the wings fell off, then it would stand to reason that a successful design for a craft that wanted to do that sort of maneuver would not be able to have wings, right?"

Seb was confused. "But then how would the thing fly? And if you're going to do that sort of turn, how would the pilot survive? They wouldn't be able to handle those Gs."

"Who said there's a pilot inside? Bit of an assumption, right?" Mr. Morose now looked very pleased with himself.

That didn't make much sense to me. "What, like a monkey? A chimp couldn't pull those Gs either."

Now Mr. Morose looked haughty. "You're going to an Advanced Weaponry base and you don't know about drones?"

"Ah, good point," allowed Seb.

"And what about the UFOs disappearing and then reappearing immediately, going the other way?" I asked.

He shrugged. "I don't have all the answers," he said. "But I'll tell you what. Either the machine moved through space and time to change direction so suddenly or, for whatever reason, the people watching them couldn't see them while they moved."

Seb frowned. "Like an invisibility cloak. But that would still mean that something without wings or engines did a 180 at 20Gs."

"Or," he said, ignoring Seb, "or the machine didn't go through time and space."

Me and Seb sat there a little dumbfounded.

Mr. Morose looked up and seemed to recognize someone on the far side of the bar. Their appearance apparently was not welcome. "Ah... If you will excuse me, I have to go now."

"Is your flight leaving?" asked Seb.

"My time here is done."

He left and I watched him go, thinking about what he had said. He was met rather roughly by a pair of men at the entrance to the bar. They were wearing nondescript black suits and walked him down the concourse away from the bar. I mentally shrugged and went back to drinking. Just another conversation between strangers travelling from one place to another, momentarily occupying the same location and sharing stories.

A game of ice hockey came onto the TV behind the bar and we settled in to watch. Seb and I both played beer league ice hockey for the same team. Seb had gotten into the sport as an adult and I had played socially for a little longer but a badly reset broken leg had gotten in the way of my skating. I kept at it for the social side and because it was fun, and it was about the only thing that got me out of the house.

I was between programming jobs but the market for my skills was robust so I didn't expect to be without a paycheck for long. Seb, on the other hand, was an enigma. He was a journalist but had come over from England under something of a cloud and would never talk about those days back in his homeland. I didn't even know how long ago that was, to tell the truth. All I knew was that he liked a drink and played good defense on the ice, and that there was always the air of him having a scheme or dodgy situation waiting in the wings about him. He always had a great story too!

A bunch of beers later and someone was tapping me on the shoulder. When I turned around, the barman was standing with a bemused grin. "I think they're paging you now," he said. I grabbed Seb and we dashed across to the gate, throwing apologies to the gate staff as we scanned our boarding passes and got on the plane. Damn near had a giggling fit through the safety briefing to many angry stares from the air hostesses. Or whatever they called themselves these days. Seb kept the buzz going with a stealthily pilfered selection of mini bottles from the drinks cart. The taxi ride at the other end was a drunken blur, as was checking into the hotel. The minibar may or may not have been given a work over, then we hit the hay.

I was much less happy in the morning. I'd given up regular heavy drinking after leaving university many moons ago, and it's a skill which really needs constant practice. It was a very somber breakfast. I knew it was going to be a long day and that the only way to soak up the alcohol would be to eat something substantial but the smell of the bacon nearly had me heaving into the buffet. But I forced myself to eat, slowly and painfully. Opposite me, Seb did his best 'Weekend at Bernie's' impression, sunglasses on and mouth slightly agape. I wasn't sure if he was asleep or sitting there awake but stupefied.

The Discovery

The package deal included a town car whose driver was not best pleased that we were late meeting him in the lobby of the hotel. He made up a little of the time on the highway but was in a foul mood when he dropped us off at the gatehouse of the base, leaving in a squeal of tires for his next pickup. A bored sentry in the guard box watched us. We blearily staggered up to him and told him who we were.

"Do you have some ID?" he asked.

Seb handed over his press credentials and was checked off the list. When I handed over my driver's license, there was the inevitable pause and query. "This is ID for a Peter Collins. The name I have on my list is for Phil Collins."

"Yeah, I go by Phil Collins but my birth name is Peter."

He frowned. "You go by a famous person's name instead of your own?"

I sighed. This happened every time I brushed against bureaucracy. "It's a nickname that stuck."

In ice hockey you submit a team list to the officials which includes all the players and their jersey numbers. They usually just have the first initial and surname so when one of my first teams were looking through the list, they decided that P Collins had to mean Phil Collins. Just as a joke, of course. But the guys on the team started to call me Phil and it stuck. Since then, I was Phil for everything except things requiring ID.

"You were supposed to be here an hour ago," he said as he checked us off from a list of names on a clipboard and picked up a phone. Moments later, a Humvee, all wide wheelbase and threatening posture, roared up and a harried looking soldier got out of the driver's side and sprinted around to meet us. He hopped from one foot to another anxiously.

"Are you Seb and Phil?"

Seb took a second to answer before nodding. "Yeah."

"Pleased to meet you. I'm Private O'Regan. Could I ask you to please get in the vehicle? We're way behind the rest of the group and we need to make up some time." He opened the door and we shuffled inside.

C. G. Lambert

Almost as soon as the door slammed shut, he'd seemingly teleported into the driver's seat and with a lurch, we accelerated smartly down the road. Over the din of the engine noise, O'Regan tried to give us a briefing of sorts but I wondered how much Seb actually took in. The road started off quite smooth but before too long, we'd gone onto a rougher track and the jostling and bumping gave Seb's paleness a green tinge. It was a relief when we screeched to a halt not long later without either of us having thrown up. I was feeling okay but still a lot less than 100%. Call it a solid 15%.

We were ushered out and to a long low building, open on one side and with windows on the other, sort of like a shooting range. We took up our station at the far end and looked through the little window. There was a bench in front with binoculars and some bottles of water. The other stations were taken up by groups of four or five civilians with a soldier for each of them. There had been no other vehicles parked out front, so it seemed like everyone else had walked some way to get here. Our soldier gestured out the window. Far in the distance on the left-hand side, an armored vehicle had parked, facing the very lightly wooded space before a wooden cabin.

"We're watching a demonstration of the small unit tactics of the future," he said. "Before us is a modified M2 Bradley Armored

Fighting Vehicle. It has a turret with a 25mm cannon, TOW anti-tank missiles and a machine gun. It has a crew of three: a tank commander, driver and gunner. The original version had space for six soldiers in the back but that has been replaced with a command center and space for two soldiers: an operational commander and systems specialist. The rest of the space is used to transport the six RC3 robotic units, four armed with our new XM7 rifles and two with the XM250 Squad Assault Weapon."

Seb was intently concentrating on opening the water bottle so I went over and helped myself to the binoculars.

"Standard deployment is for the SysSpec to release four mini drones to survey the operational area."

I turned to him. "Won't they get shot down?"

He smiled. "They're the size of a baseball. They move pretty quickly and they're scanning the area with infrared and hi-res cameras. All that information gets fed back to the SysSpec and assembled on computer screens that display a 3D view of the environment for the OpCom to use to make informed decisions. The RC3s then deploy out the back of the Bradley and approach the target. Watch."

I turned my attention to the scene. The ramp at the back of the Bradley had indeed lowered and the RC3s came out. They looked a lot like the Robot dogs from Boston Dynamics. Like a robot the size and proportions of a greyhound but without the neck and head. On its back sat an arm with some sort of box on it, like a mini missile launcher.

"The RC3's XM7s are incorporated in a chassis which allows the recoil to be minimized, and includes a high-res camera which also feeds back to the Bradley. They each carry 500 rounds of ammunition which is a lot more than the standard deployment of regular soldiers of 6+1."

"6+1?"

"Six magazines in the webbing and one in the weapon. 140 rounds. The standard load out for a XM250 is 400 rounds but each of our RC3s takes 1000."

"Wow. All that ammunition sounds great but how good are they at shooting?" I pointed at the dog with a larger box on its back. "Surely those machine guns will bounce around a lot?"

"The techs are still working on that but they're there more for suppression than sniping. The XM7 carbines are much more accurate and their cameras are much more hi-res."

"And the dogs - the RC3s, they move around okay? Wouldn't the terrain cause them to trip or fall? Why not have tracked vehicles?"

In response, the soldier gestured.

I got the binoculars up in time to see the RC3s approaching the log cabin. They moved smoothly over the undulating terrain, and did not seem to get caught on any of the bushes or tree roots.

"How do they see?"

"They have sensors built into the chassis which are constantly scanning the ground in front of them for where to put their feet. They're good on all terrain. Tracked vehicles are heavier and therefore we can't carry as many in the AFV. Tracked vehicles don't quite have the same issues with recoil as these ones do but they get bogged down in sand."

Private O'Regan handed me an iPad. On it, I could see a top-down map of the area, with the Bradley showing as a small rectangle on the left-hand side and the hut as a block of color on the right. The map wasn't satellite imagery as the trees were mostly transparent and even the roof of the hut was a mere suggestion. The map looked like it was being constantly updated, as if four or five people were constantly drawing the scene from a slightly different angle. Where they agreed, the lines were solid but where they didn't, the lines were thinner and less sure. Like a computer game really. The imagery obviously included infrared because the

Bradley had five heat signatures and the hut had ten, and I turned to Private O'Regan. "Does the hut have actual people in there?"

He shook his head. "No, they're heat sources to replicate people. We don't want to waste any of our own troops."

Seb had managed to work out how to open the bottle and had drained it noisily. "Why not just have a couple of snipers - or even better, sniper robots and take the baddies out from afar? Don't you have those 50-cal rifles that can punch through concrete?"

Private Dan nodded. "Yeah, the M107. But the 25mm is twice the size and carries a mix of rounds - HiEx, AP and even the Depleted Uranium rounds. So if you need heavy support, the Bradley can deliver. It looks like the assault is beginning," Private Dan said, gesturing with his chin.

He showed me how to navigate on the iPad and now I could see the camera feed coming in from the individual RC3s. "Hey, this is really good footage," I told him. I had seen police and combat footage from chest cams before and it was inevitably shaky; the cameras always pointed at the ground when the wearer took cover and you never saw enough wide shots to contextualize what the hell was going on. A good analogy for combat in general perhaps.

"The signal is run through a stabilizer program after it reaches the Bradley. We're taking the feed off the Bradley rather than directly from the RC3s."

Four of the RCs appeared as blue squares and the other two as triangles. I watched as they stalked forward, alternating between following them on the map and peering through the window to see first-hand what was going on. As the hut came into view, one of the triangles stopped moving and on the first-person camera, I could see that it had zoomed in so that the hut filled the frame. The RCs seemed to have moved up in two squads, each centered around one of the triangles.

"We would never do that with flesh soldiers," said O'Regan, indicating the splitting of the forces. "See how they are coming at the hut from almost opposite sides?"

Seb got it immediately. "If there's any shooting, you risk hitting each other."

A thought occurred to me. "If you have to go room to room, don't flesh soldiers usually have grenades? Like flashbangs or something? Or even tear gas?"

Private O'Regan nodded. "The tech guys are working on that. They initially tried bolting on the smoke grenade systems that the tanks use but that was overkill, and way too cumbersome. The civilian version of the dogs comes with an arm in the middle of the back, so there were some thoughts on bolting that on and having it throw grenades around. They'll figure it out but we're not quite there yet. Besides, the RC3s can just charge in and shoot the enemy. They can take a round or two in exchange." He gestured towards the tablet. "Keep watching," he said.

On one of the cameras, a flash of movement was detected at one of the windows - a stick with a rag on it waving like someone walking in front of the window. Immediately, the wood around the window turned into a spray of wood chips and a second later, the sound of automatic fire reached us. It shut off pretty quickly – only a quick burst. A couple of minutes later, the map showed that the RC3s were making their way inside the hut. I couldn't get the binoculars retrained quickly enough to catch the robots entering but the rattle of short bursts echoing across the sparse forest indicated that they had gone in. The heat signatures on the iPad had spilled and splashes of hot liquid were making their way across the floor.

I turned to O'Regan, a bit concerned. "Those weren't actually people were they?"

"No," he said. More bored than amused. "Those are heated sacks of blood. In hostage scenarios, we want to check for accuracy.

Nothing shows injuries like the bags - ricochets, splinters, stray shots and shrapnel all pop the bag. They make you careful."

Some of the other groups of press and VIPs were talking with their Army liaisons but a lot more were heading away from our low-slung building, heading out along the path that led out the other side.

"The others are heading to the next point by foot where their transport is waiting but because we were so late, we had to park closer to the entrance to this particular field. So we will need to head back to the Humvee and drive around to the next field instead."

I looked over at the shambling corpse that was Seb. He looked how I felt. Another trip in the Humvee on the uneven ground sounded like a recipe for disaster. Walking wasn't much better but at least we could walk slowly. "How about we walk and meet you there?"

Private O'Regan shook his head decisively. "I'm afraid that is out of the question. I am required to accompany you at all times and we have to retrieve the Humvee now. Please follow me."

He led us back to the Humvee and we reluctantly reboarded and tried to settle ourselves in for the drive.

About ten minutes later, the jiggling and bumping got too much for Seb. "Pull over, I'm going to be sick!" he blurted. O'Regan screeched to a halt and Seb managed to get out and made it to a tree before the heaving started. The contents of my own water bottle made its presence known and I headed in the other direction to find a tree of my own. O'Regan didn't even notice, focusing on getting more water for Seb.

I was lost in the rapture of being momentarily ignored by my hangover while the pressure on my bladder was slowly and ecstatically releasing when I glanced up at the branch of the tree I was leaned against and noticed a palm-sized patch of fabric partially embedded in the bark of the tree. I stared at it vacantly, not really seeing it at all. Eventually my bladder was empty and I got myself sorted and turned to return to the hummer. As an afterthought, I reached back and took the scrap of fabric and placed it into my pocket.

By the time I got back to the hummer, Seb had finished what he was doing and was rinsing his mouth with the water from the bottle that Private O'Regan had given him. He led the way back to the Humvee and we resumed our trip, a little more gently this time. The scrap of fabric stayed in my pocket, largely forgotten throughout the rest of the day of watching high tech warfare. It stayed in my pocket on the trip home after the visit in the taxi back to the airport. It made it through security and onto the plane and stayed forgotten in my pocket until Seb and I both rolled into our flat.

The Suit

I'm embarrassed to say that the scrap of fabric remained in my pocket for another week after that. I was... between jobs at that point. We had a three-bedroom house on the border of a light industrial zone within walking distance of the local ice rink. Handy for me and Seb to walk to games and practices, and close enough for Andrew, our other flatmate, to cycle to his work.

The house was a little on the old side, nothing breaking down or anything, just a little run down. Back when it was first built, there was supposed to be a big residential subdivision going in adjacent to the semi-industrial area. But the zoning changed and so the infrastructure to support the new houses never got installed and as a result, we weren't on the gas lines. So, it was electricity for heating and cooking. Rent was cheap which was convenient for me as I had been laid off a month before. I was lucky enough to have gotten a nice pay out of six months' salary in exchange for being downsized due to a 'change in company direction.' I was super grateful - tech layoffs are almost never that generous. I'd heard a horror story of a firm that wanted to do a round of layoffs. They held a fire drill and when everyone was milling around the assembly points, they told everyone that if their security pass worked when it came to getting back into the office, then they still had a job. If not? That was just too bad.

I was living frugally as I applied for jobs to try and stretch that payout as long as possible. We're talking about microwaved burritos and two-minute rice with a boil-in-the-bag vegetable pack. I was also stretching the time between laundry loads to save on laundry powder, and so it was a week later that I was emptying my jeans pockets and found the scrap of fabric from the visit to the high-tech military base. I was in the utility room loading the washing machine when I found it and absent mindedly put it on the bench beside the washing machine as I attended to the laundry and again promptly forgot about it.

"Phil, what's this?" asked Andrew. Andrew had a sweet job, working a strict 9 to 5 doing god knows what for one of those big research labs, and by all accounts getting paid a pretty penny to do it too. He was ten years younger than me and Seb, and very much the opposite of us. Whereas I was relaxed about my career progression and Seb saw his job as an excuse to party, Andrew was diligent and hard working. Seb and I naturally deferred to him in terms of morning routines, seeing as he had office hours and places to be at a particular time. He, in turn, was understanding when we hung up our hockey gear to dry in the utility room after a game or practice. The system worked well.

I wandered back to the utility room to see if the wash cycle had not finished in time for him to use it. He was leaning against the wall, turning the fabric over and over in his hands. "Is this yours?" he asked.

"Sure," I said breezily. "What is it?"

He looked up and smiled. "You don't know what it is?"

I shrugged. "I found it." I waited. He seemed quite interested in it.

"Do you mind if I run it under one of the microscopes at work? It feels strange."

"What do you mean, strange?"

"Strange. Like when you put your finger close to a tablet or phone screen. You know, when your body's electromagnetic field triggers the machine."

I frowned. I hadn't felt anything when I had picked it up. Although I had been hung over, admittedly. I reached out for it and when Andrew placed it in my hand, I could see what he meant. Like a slight fuzziness.

I shrugged. "Sure. Do some tests if you like. I don't mind. Let me know what you find."

I left him there, turning it over in his hand, staring at it intently.

Fast forward three days to the weekend. It was a respectful 10am and Seb still hadn't come home from his Friday night but that wasn't unusual at all. I was in the lounge watching the replays of the ice hockey game featuring my second favorite team from the night before, and Andrew came out of his room and headed to the kitchen for breakfast. He sat down beside me with his bowl of cereal. "You got a minute?"

I paused the game and turned to him. "Sure, what's up?"

He hesitated before answering, the spoon in his mouth and his eyes focusing on something in the middle of the lounge. He got like that sometimes. He was a bit of a loner; he never had any friends over, and had never had a girlfriend for the time we'd known him. He wasn't a total introvert - you could talk with him and he'd have a drink now and again, but he was definitely dancing to the beat of his own drum.

"I ran some tests on that scrap of fabric you gave me."

"Ah, cool. What was it?"

He paused again. Fuck, this was going to take forever if I had to drag it out of him. "I was very interested in how such a small scrap could behave like a phone screen."

I nodded.

"And it can't. It doesn't read the electromagnetic field of your finger like a screen does."

"Okay..."

"I did some experiments and it's more like a force field. Well, it would be for a whole sheet of the material. It seems that if you had a whole lot of it, then it would stop items with high kinetic energy from ever reaching someone on the other side of the material."

"So, like a bullet proof screen?"

"Yeah like that. But even better."

"How so?"

"A bullet proof vest works by physically stopping the bullet and taking as much of the energy as it can out of the bullet. It's not perfect at that, so some of the energy gets through. You see that in the movies where people get shot and fall over, and have these big bruises. Enough energy gets through to make the bruise and to make everybody think that they've been killed. This is different. The fabric makes a field which converts the kinetic energy of the bullet into electrical power that goes into the fabric. So by the time the bullet touches the fabric, all of the kinetic energy has been converted and the speed of the bullet is zero. So it would just fall down."

I rubbed my jaw as I thought about it. "That would be a great bulletproof suit because it could cover your face. I never knew why movie baddies didn't shoot the hero in the body to get them down and then follow up with two to the head, just to make sure. No vest is going to stop that."

"That's true but there's more. The material has a field, true. But the construction of the fabric is super interesting. I had to get out some of the specialized equipment in the lab to check this out but if you zoom in enough, you can see that the fabric is made up of super fine fibers that act like muscles."

"Huh?"

Andrew put the spoon back in his bowl of cereal. "What do you know about muscles?"

I looked down at my paunch and frowned at him to see if he was mocking me. He didn't notice the gesture but continued his lecture.

"Muscles are just bundles of fibers which contract when they get an electrical message from the brain. We have luckily worked out how to contract the right groups of muscles in the right sequences to do things like walk, run, talk and eat without having to think about all of the minute muscle groups that have to be triggered at just the right time for them to work in concert."

"Ah, okay."

"And if you look closely enough, this fabric mimics the behavior of those muscles."

"But that bit of fabric was tiny. How powerfully could those fibers contract? Are we talking about adding a little bit of a lift to your step or are we talking about being able to jump over a building?"

"Normally I'd agree - the material is thin and while the fibers don't seem to be hard to replicate, there aren't many of them. So I naturally thought that they would not be able to do much. So I tested it. If my calculations are correct, then we're talking about human level strength if we made the fabric a half inch thick."

"But you just finished saying that humans have already figured out how to piece together which muscle has to fire and when to make us walk and run and such. So will this fabric magically know how to do all that?"

"Oh, no. Someone would have to program all that stuff in but I don't think that you understand the implications."

I blinked. To be fair, Andrew had had a lot more time to think about this than I had.

"Think of all the life-saving applications. Airbags. Airplane safety. Bulletproof vests."

I looked up at the TV. The puck had been dumped into the corner and I had accidentally paused just when the winger and defenseman had come together while contesting it. "Or protecting against getting crunched in the corner," I said, while indicating the action on the TV.

Andrew noticed for the first time what was on the TV. "I... guess."

"Wow, that would be awesome."

"I'm sorry... what does that mean?"

"Collisions happen in any sport. In football, you have a tackle or a block. In soccer, you have a tackle. In ice hockey, you have a check. There are all these rules about who you can hit and when and how you do it. It's the one benefit a big guy like me has. You have more energy to put into the hit."

Andrew nodded. He got it. "Force equals mass times acceleration."

"Sure, okay. But if you have a field? A field which arrests anything approaching and changes their energy to zero, then you negate the effects of their check. So you'd be able to skate around without worrying about being hit."

"And that's a big deal on the ice?"

"Well, it's not the be-all and end-all but it's something." I considered the players on the screen. "Could you make a suit? Can you make more of the fabric?"

"I could try. I'll have a look after work. There's some clever approaches when you zoom in..."

My eyes glazed over as he explained using intricate finger motions to demonstrate some examples. The very beginnings of a plan of my own were percolating in the deepest parts of my brain.

A few weeks went by before he presented the suit to me. I wish I could tell you that it was a glistening black futuristic suit that a superhero would be proud of but instead it was a cobbled together patchwork of different shades. I held it up and looked it up and down.

He looked defensive. "Hey, it was hard to get the materials. I needed to get the leftover resin from different jobs, and even when the resin says that it's black, there are lots of different shades of black. I had to..." My eyes glazed over as he explained the difficulties.

I focused instead on the suit. It would probably fit. I turned it over in my hands until something he said snapped me back to the present.

"Sorry, say that again."

"Yeah, I thought that would impress you. The suit itself can store the energy that it extracts from arresting things that are flying at it."

"Ah, ok. I thought that was something important."

"It is important!"

"Okay. Why is it important? What does it mean?"

"It means you can program the suit to move on its own."

"Wow..."

"Yeah, wow. It needs a little battery to get started. But the material is incredibly efficient. There are enough of those fibers I was telling you about to give the suit the ability to stand on its own two feet... if it had feet. Then you can see how the field-arresting motion can combine with the self-powering of the suit to recharge itself so then it can just keep going and going."

"I'm sorry. Again, in English?"

He picked up the spoon and used it to emphasize his point. "You have an impact event."

"A check."

"A check. Right. It recharges the battery."

"I'm sorry, you say that the suit can do its own thing?"

"Yes."

"So I could put it on, and it could run and jump and I wouldn't get tired?"

"Well, eventually you might. Your muscles would be powering your motion so you would get fatigued by that." He thought for a second. "But you would have to be very careful with the instructions you give the suit because if you said that your hips could twist past a certain point which your anatomy couldn't support, then the suit would basically wrench your leg off. How good are you at programming?"

I smiled. "I'm good enough."

"Seriously. You need like three or four layers of safety because whoever is in the suit could be killed. Literally."

"Okay, I got it. You don't want to program it yourself?"

He gave me his best Scotty impression from Star Trek. "Dammit Captain, I'm a scientist, not a programmer."

I snorted. "Okay, fine. I guess that's on me then."

"I assume you will be programming it for ice hockey?"

I tried not to say 'Duh!' "Of course!"

"So you'll need data for that."

"What kind of data?"

"Biomechanical data. Which joints need to rotate how many degrees, that sort of thing. Which muscles twitch when you take a stride."

Again, this guy was a half-step ahead of me. "I guess so."

"Where will you get that?"

"I don't know. Maybe Seb will have some thoughts."

Andrew snorted. "Yeah, he usually does."

"Hey, thanks for this."

"Yeah, no worries. If you get asked where you got it, don't mention my name alright?"

"Sure of course," I said. But I was already miles away, planning data structures and interfaces in my mind.

The Team

The ice hockey rink was a nondescript building in a semi-industrial area nestled between a green belt and the fringes of an affordable housing development. It followed the typical layout of bleachers on one side with the changing rooms underneath. On the other side of the ice surface were the administrative areas, as well as Zamboni storage, a cafe, pro shop and first aid room. The prime rental times were taken up with public skating sessions and the second tier of convenient times had figure skating and learn to skate classes, leaving the various ice hockey teams and leagues to fight over what was left. So, it wasn't unusual to have a midweek 11pm game or a practice scheduled for 7am.

Somehow, our league had snaffled the two slots straight after the public skating session on Saturday nights for our games. Each game was an hour of running time - two fifteen-minute periods, two five-minute breaks between periods, and a twenty-minute final period. I made it to the rink about forty minutes before the game started and found which of the four changing rooms we would be in. I wasn't the first of the guys there - Jeremy the goalie was in the corner about halfway dressed in his gear, and Dave had also just arrived.

"How many do we have tonight?" I asked Dave, nodding a hello to Jeremy.

He found a spot on the bench near the entrance to the shower. It was a coveted spot because most of the space in the changing rooms was under the seats above and so had limited head room. "We should have ten or eleven skaters tonight - maybe twelve if George can get out early."

You would start the season with as close to an ideal roster of nine forwards, six defense and a goalie as you could get, but the number of players who would actually turn up for games and practices was randomly determined by the various demands on their time from work, school and family. Apart from Jeremy, the position they needed you to play would depend on who turned up. Oh, and if our goalie didn't show up, we were screwed. It was a specialist position so not one that just anyone could jump into. Nobody really wanted to get suited up just to watch a game serving as a backup, so you usually only had the one goalie.

The rest of the guys trickled into the changing rooms. Dave was a doctor, Dean was a pilot and Dan was a dope head. Benji was an architect and Pete was a fitter for a yacht maker. The big yachts. He'd been playing for long enough for his son to be old enough to play with us.

The diversity in occupations was matched only by the broad range of ages, body shapes and experience levels, which made for some interesting work stories. Brent was a builder and with his powerful build and long straggly hair, he could have been cast as a cave man. When he came in, he sat beside me on the bench beneath the bleachers above.

"So the Police say that the guy can't press charges after all." That attracted the attention of the room.

"Huh?" I asked.

"Oh, that's right, you missed that story. You know how my truck kept getting broken into and my tools kept getting stolen?"

I nodded. I had heard that side of things at least.

"Well, we had that early morning slot last week and so I had put my gear ready to go just outside my bedroom. But in the middle of the night, I heard someone messing with my truck so I jumped up and ran out, and grabbed one of my sticks as I went past. The clown stood up and came at me when I got down there. He had a hatchet on him but I think he was expecting me to be scared off at the sight of it when he started waving it around. But I was sick of having to get new tools every week and having to replace my truck window or door, so I was pissed. I chopped him in the leg and he went down and then I started wailing on him, and messed him up good. They had to take him to hospital and the cops at the time tried to tell me that he might press charges. But I just heard that they think that will be a waste of time, so all is good."

"He's lucky you didn't have a gun. Or hey, you could have messed him up big time with a nail gun."

"What's that smell?"

Everyone started sniffing the air. One thing about hockey gear is that you sweat in it and if you don't air it out between games, it can develop a certain personality of its own. The smell in question was more of a cleaning product or bleach smell though. Matty, one of our defenseman who could have been a model with those sharp cheekbones and tall angular body, looked a bit bashful.

"Yeah, that's me guys. We've got new kittens and they hate the smell of my gear. So when it's out drying, they come over and pee on it. I've scrubbed the pee smell out of it but now it smells like a cleaning cupboard instead."

Some of the suggested solutions for training the kittens out of that behavior were best left to your imagination and in general, whenever you get a locker full of guys, the tone of the conversations goes downhill in a hurry.

Before we knew it, the Zamboni was out on the ice indicating that there was maybe five minutes before we started, and it was time to figure out the lines. Dave went through the team list assigning the pairs and I ended up with Penfold as my other winger. There were two approaches to pairing people: you could try and get the best players together to maximize the playing ability on the ice, knowing that you'd end up with a weaker line as well, or you could try and balance the lines. I couldn't figure out which way Dave was going with this coupling as I was middling and a little better than Penfold. It certainly wasn't a problem though, I was happy to play with any of the guys, but typically if you got less able players together, you would get them to concentrate on the defensive side of the game. I figured that was our role, so as we shuffled from the changing rooms out to the bench, I told Penfold that we were the checking line. The Zamboni was just finishing up and George came jogging gently back to the bench to get his skates on, having just finished his cigarette.

The other approach to line management was to give the lines with the best players the most ice time. Our team wasn't like that - everybody paid the same amount of money per year so we just rolled the lines. Everybody got the same amount of ice time. We played running time so the clock started and kept going until the end of the period regardless of penalties or game stoppages. It was the only way the rink could fit all the games in an evening. And if you were unlucky and only a few players could make the game then you might be looking at only one or two guys on the bench and so you got a lot of ice time. Each shift would be nowhere near the goal of forty-five to sixty seconds, but measured in minutes. The funniest game I had was when we had a short bench and players would try to change only to be sent back out by an unfit player who would gasp, "I've only just come off!"

My line was doing a good defensive job. When you're playing, you want to do well for your teammates. You don't want to let them down. So when you're going into the corners, you dig extra hard to try and win the puck and when the opposition is coming through the neutral zone, you bust your ass skating to try and break up their attack. Penfold made up for the lack of natural ability with dogged determination and good positioning.

As the game progressed, our two centers (who, remember, were playing half the game each) began to tire and play more conservatively, staying high. Penfold and I on the other hand were playing every third shift, so we had more gas in the tank. So we stepped up our forechecking, energetically chasing down the puck whenever our opponents had it. The score was tied and we were halfway through the third period when it happened. Our defenseman got the puck, got to the red line and shot the puck into the zone. Their defenseman went back to collect the puck, and I was right behind him, breathing down his neck. He managed to get to it first and forced a pass up to their winger waiting for it at the hash marks with his butt against the boards. I could see that Penfold was closing on their winger but the assumption was that the winger would get an outlet pass out to their center who would carry the puck out of their zone. Somehow though, Penfold managed to lift their winger's stick and get control of the puck. I was mid stride trying to close on the opposition to break up their counter attack but noticed that Penfold had managed to secure the puck, so I slammed on the brakes. Penfold saw me and made a tape-to-tape pass.

I had stopped on one foot with my entire weight loaded on that skate, leaning to my left. When the puck popped out and landed on my blade, I was already in the process of transferring my weight from my right to left leg, so when I shot the puck, it had all my weight behind it. Totally unlike me. The puck magically disappeared over the goalkeeper's shoulder into the net. From the bench and the stands, it looked like Penfold and I had pulled off some sort of set play with a professional level snipe to score the go-ahead goal. My teammates on the ice converged on me to congratulate me on the goal. "'Checking line'," Penfold snorted.

Arguably the best part of the game was the beer afterwards. That was when you sat half changed out of your pads and savored the shared experiences of the game. And when you gave and received good natured ribbing for the decisions you made on the ice or commiserated on being handcuffed, receiving the puck all alone in front of the goalie and not able to get the shot away.

One of our new guys noticed Matty's shoulder pads hanging by a single rivet. "Aw jeez, they look like they're on their last legs, eh?"

He grinned. "Nah, that rivet broke the second game I got them and they've been going strong for fifteen seasons since. If the other rivet ever went, I think it might be time to hang up the skates. It would be a sign!"

By and large, gear tended to be well worn and repaired, sometimes mismatched. If the palm of one of your gloves wore through and couldn't be repaired, would you throw away the other glove as well? And when team colors changed for whatever reason, there would be a sizable outlay for a home and away jersey plus matching socks. As one player said, "If I buy another hockey jersey, my wife will kill me!" You can imagine that after playing hockey for forty years, you would accumulate a fair number of jerseys.

After shooting the shit with the guys after the game, I stood up to leave and hit my head on the underside of the seats above. Every fricken time!

The Data

"Explain it to me again," said Seb pensively.

I sighed. "Let me try it this way. The suit is made up of little squares, all stitched together. In each square are fibers, like thin threads. If I send an electrical impulse to the threads, then they shorten. Like a lot. If I then turn off the electricity, the thread relaxes."

Now Seb was nodding. He was finally getting it. "Like a muscle, right?"

"Right. So I've got a million threads and I've sorted them so they're in groups depending on which part of the body they are covering."

"Okay, so your computer program knows which threads are wrapped around your left thigh, for example."

"Excellent! Yes. But now comes my problem. Skating is not just saying to your body 'twitch left thigh now'. It's a complex series of muscle contractions coupled with feedback from the body's balance system. The good news is that I have the parts working independently. The suit can detect my motion while I'm wearing it, and taking a basic stride is relatively straight forward in terms of which bits of the suit twitches when. But the suit still doesn't really know how to skate. It doesn't know what series of muscle movements are required. The suit doesn't know the basic stuff that you learn when learning to skate, and that you train your body to know how to do it by practicing it over and over again. It's just data."

Seb's furrowed brow relaxed as the penny dropped. "I think I get it. That makes sense. Do you know anyone who would have that data?"

Now it was my turn to be frustrated. I'd racked my brain and came up with one answer. "The only people I can think of are computer game developers. They put those little ping pong balls on a skater and then get them to skate, pass and check while recording them. Then they digitize that data so then they can animate them in the computer game."

Seb nodded. "Right and how would we go about getting that data off them?"

I shrugged. "We could try and buy it from them, I guess."

Seb looked skeptical. "Maybe. But realistically, the only people who would also need that data would be someone else making an ice hockey computer game. Would you sell your secret data to a competitor? They might not want to share that data at any price."

He was right. "And we couldn't tell them that we were making a figure skating game because they might not give us the puck handling, passing, shooting and checking movement data, right?"

"Yeah, so buying it might not be an option."

I stared into my beer as if the answer might be in there somewhere. A change in the atmosphere of the room made me look up. Seb wasn't sharing my despondent outlook. He looked like he had thought of something. But the look on his face was the one that usually presaged a plan which would end up being illegal, immoral or both.

"What are you thinking?"

He smiled an evil grin. "Well if they won't sell it to us, maybe we can steal the data?"

"Oh boy." I said. "Here we go."

An hour later, we had a list of the companies who had released at least one ice hockey computer game and where they were based. We had a list of offices for those computer game companies. We also had a list of events that the companies ran where they invited people into their offices for whatever reason. Talks on HR initiatives, products they used, awards evenings; it was surprising how much they were involved in promoting the idea that they were a good place to work.

"So even if we can make it into the office, how will we find out where they store the data files and how will we get access to them?"

"Well, won't they have a server room somewhere where we can get access and then find the data and download it all onto a thumb drive?"

"Maybe, if this was the last century."

He blinked as if I had slapped him. "Huh?"

"You're asking if they will have a room in the building somewhere which will have rack upon rack of computers and we'll be able to get into the room and log on to one of the boxes and track down the files. Then we'll be able to plug a thumb drive into that machine and load those files onto it before logging off and slipping out of the room?"

He literally pouted. "Well, that's what they do in the movies."

I sighed as I nodded, allowing that movies grossly misrepresented how software development worked these days. "Right, not your fault. Here's what's way more likely. They do everything in the cloud. So the actual files are at Google or Amazon or Azure or maybe in their own data center, but that's not going to be on-site. It'll be in the bowels of a purpose-built facility out in the middle of nowhere. To get access to it, we could go there ourselves but that would be a waste of time because we would have no way of knowing which of their hundreds of thousands of identical black boxes holds the data that we want. The good news is that there would be three or four backups: one in the same facility, one in a facility somewhere else in the country and one on the other side of the world. Just in case one of their hard drives fail. So we would be much better served getting access to their files from their office. Using a login and password that we somehow get from one of their employees."

"What, we ring them up and say that we're from their IT department and they should give us their username and password?"

"That's called phishing."

"Fishing?"

"Phishing with a 'ph'. Yeah, that's not going to work on a few levels. IT teams are specifically training their staff against phishing attacks. Plus if we were IT, we wouldn't need their access details for a cloud provider. So that's not going to work either."

"So how do we get the data? Do we have to cut off someone's finger or gouge out an eyeball to pass biometric security?"

I looked at him closely to see if he was serious. Sometimes I wondered about him. "Err... I don't think so..."

Andrew joined us for a beer, slumping on the couch beside us. "What are we talking about? Who's playing?"

Seb emptied his can, paused the game that had been playing in the background and got up to get another drink. "We're planning a heist. Do you want to join us?"

Andrew sipped his drink. "What's the score? Diamonds? Bullion?"

Seb took a long draught of his beer before answering. "Data." He burped. "Biomechanical data."

Andrew frowned. "Sounds like a lot of risk for not much reward. Why do you need biomechanical data?"

We explained about programming the suit. He stared at us in disbelief. Seb started to elaborate before Andrew cut him off. "No, no, I get it. But you already have all the biomechanical data you could ever hope for. You don't need to travel and risk breaking and entering to get it."

I looked at him, not understanding what he was saying. Seb was equally flummoxed. Andrew pointed at the TV. "You can set up image recognition and run hours of video through it. Program it to find the elbows and knees and heads of the players and then work out the posture and positions of the players frame by frame. You'll have incredibly detailed data about every player and how they skate, and what each part of the body does every step of the way."

We pondered that. "But won't the camera angles be too far away?"

"It really doesn't matter. You train the AI to detect the points that it's interested in, no matter what kind of camera shot it is, and also to recognize the player that it's measuring. You'll be able to see where the forces are being applied to the ice and where the balance points are."

I blinked, realizing that he was right. It would mean more programming, but I had everything I needed.

"That's great! Brilliant! And if the code recognizes which player is which, then I can isolate particular players and see how they skate to make sure I model the program on the best skaters."

"So the suit will mimic what the best players do and you'll be wearing it, so you will be doing what those best players do?"

The way he said that made me pause in my glee. "Uh... yes?"

"Okay, don't take this the wrong way, but... what if your body can't do what the programming says it needs to?"

"We covered that - the suit is also like built in muscles, so my body doesn't need to be able to do the—"

"Not quite what I mean. You're tall, right? So what happens if you program the suit to act like you're six foot instead of six foot four? Will your legs get shorter because of the programming? No. If it decides, after you train it on footage of someone who is 6 foot 9 like that defenseman Zdeno Chara, that your stride should be *this* long because your leg should be *this* long, how is that going to impact your body?"

I thought about this for a minute. Everyone is differently proportioned and in ice hockey, people with longer legs tended to be better skaters because the same amount of energy expended translates to more distance covered for those with longer legs. Which was a pity because if good skaters had 60/40 leg to torso proportions, I was more like 30/70. Stumpy legs on a long body. Whatever programming I did was going to have to find a way to take the performance of athletes with very different heights, weights, strengths and body proportions, and work out how to best drive my body around the ice, as well as take shots and passes, without my body needing to have a particular size or shape.

Fortunately, I didn't have a job to go to and I had a passion for the subject, so I knew that the next few weeks were going to be filled

C. G. Lambert

with me getting super knowledgeable about the biomechanics of ice hockey and how that could be translated onto a body of any size. An intellectual endeavor likely to lead to PhD-level knowledge and no way of getting full credit for it. If I published how I had made the suit or how I programmed it, there would be no way I could play in the NHL!

Training

The suit looked like a patchwork quilt of different shades of black. It was thin though, so it resembled the material they made neck guards from to prevent ice hockey players from getting cut with skate blades. I had treated the programming of the suit as an exercise in best practices and I was very happy with how it had ended up. Because it was so important, I did all the boring things that usually got left to last – testing, performance tuning and making sure that edge cases were covered. It was super robust and well tested, the best programming work that I had done.

I had taken a seriously paranoid attitude to the movements of the suit. I had done work in three dimensions before but nothing like this. This included the twisting of the model during skating, as well as having to handle movement in three dimensions while constantly referring to sensor data and keeping track of where the stick and puck were. It had been a very real challenge. The safety precautions I had programmed revolved around the maximum degrees of movement that the body in the suit, i.e. me, would have to undergo. I was not the most flexible of people and I had nightmares of wearing the suit and the programming deciding that a leg or an arm could move beyond the limits of human ability, or more worryingly, the limits of my body's ability with the freakish result of such a catastrophic failure in programming being one of my joints popping like a butcher deboning a chicken.

Some of the math behind the transformations was particularly complex, and one particular set of problems had me staring at my computer for hours before I finally admitted defeat. The solution seemed to involve a combination of Euclidean geometry and advanced arrays but I couldn't keep it straight in my head. Fortunately, I had gone to university with a guy who might be able to help.

Izmir was one of those slightly built guys with two percent body fat and a super intense look who radiated intellect. He'd gotten his undergrad degree, master's degree and PhD in the time it took me to complete my undergrad, and then stayed on at the university to teach. The last I heard in the alumni email newsletter, he was heading up a symposium on some highly theoretical branch of mathematics where physics and calculus met.

"Izmir? Peter Collins. I don't know if you remember me, we hung out at uni?"

"Yes, I remember you! How are you doing Peter?"

I briefly explained the issue I was having, and without a noticeable pause, Izmir had the solution.

"Yes, I did something similar when I was supporting one of my PhD candidates. If I remember correctly, the solution involved Frenet-Serret frames and we explored various ways of visualizing the models. We had to build an online API to connect the visualization engine with the data, just let me see if that server is still up and running... it was a while ago..." In the background, I could hear typing on a keyboard, rapid fire touch typing - "... Ah, here it is. Everything is still up and running. Tell you what, I'll forward you the link to their thesis and that should explain everything. When you come to actually include it in your work, let me know and I'll give you some credentials to check your outputs with the visualization engine. It makes it so much easier to see if you've gone wrong."

I thanked him and hung up and then spent a week exploring the link he had sent through, trying to understand it all. It was the hardest I had worked my brain in a very long time! But it was very rewarding when the data I eventually fed into the visualization engine returned sensible outputs.

The years of playing ice hockey computer games had given me a lot of ideas regarding an interface which would allow me to tweak and alter the parameters of the suit – to increase or decrease the safety factor of how many degrees this or that joint could withstand, to increase or decrease the length of stride or the speed of response to the wearer, that sort of thing. The difference between the suit and the computer games was the interaction. With the games, I would use a controller or the keyboard. Push this button for this action, hit the space bar for a shot, that sort of thing. But with the suit, the suit itself was the controller. If I wanted to turn left, I would start to turn left. The suit would detect the motion, figure out what I wanted to do and then perform it perfectly. The issue would be adjusting my body's reaction to the suit taking over the motion. My body would not be used to the motions the suit would demand or how to trigger certain moves. It was almost relearning how to skate and that was going to take some time. Hence my presence at the public skating session at the local rink.

"Hey, James!"

"Oh, hi." James was the rink manager. That basically meant that he drove the Zamboni, opened up in the morning and locked up at night. He played in the league a level above mine.

"Have you got a minute?"

"Sure, what's up?"

"How much do you guys charge for the ice?"

He told me. I groaned. That was way too much for me to be able to afford for all of the time it was going to take for me to get good at using the suit.

"That's our standard rate. Are you looking to get more practice in? If you get enough people to your sessions, it doesn't work out to be too much per player."

"It's more for just me on the ice. There's some things I want to try and I'm too embarrassed to do it in front of anyone else. So I'm looking for some time on the ice by myself where nobody will be watching."

He paused for a long moment, eyeing me suspiciously. While he was currently playing in the league above mine, we had played on some teams together in previous seasons and we went back a long way, and that history evidently tipped his decision. "Well… I'll tell you what. Yvonne is always at me with how long I spend at the rink and what keeps me here so late is having to lock up after the last session. If I taught you how to use the Zamboni and gave you a key, you could stay as long as you liked, so long as you cut the ice and locked up after yourself. What do you think?"

"That would be perfect, thanks for that man!"

"Yeah, I'm trusting you here. Nobody can stay in the rink overnight, it's not a hotel. No drinking, and you have to lock up. Our insurance won't pay out if anything happens and we don't lock up, so you'd be fucking me over if you forget."

"No, no, you can trust me."

He looked at me for a second, obviously weighing up whether he could, in fact, trust me, before nodding. "Okay, find me after the session and I'll show you the Zamboni."

Thud. Bang. Groan.

Thud. Bang. Groan.

The only sound after midnight for the next few weeks was some combination of thudding as I hit the ice, banging as I went into the boards or groaning as I recovered from the aforementioned thuds and bangs. It was exactly like my earliest lessons at the Learn to Skate classes, as I trained the suit to allow me to be able to skate, balance, turn and go backwards. Then, as the speed increased, the bladework became more intricate, as did the consequences for getting it wrong. Going from the outside edge to the inside edge of the same skate in order to flick from forwards to backwards involved some interesting crashes. One particular exercise involved me literally getting vertical before landing on my side with my arm cushioning my head as I hit the ice. I would go from 10pm to after midnight with my laptop plugged into a wall outlet for power, resting on the scorekeeper's bench while I went through whatever routine I was trying to perfect. Then I would skate over and plug in to make some slight adjustments to the programming, to one or two of the parameters, or to the safety precautions, if I thought they were stifling my progress.

Eventually, exhausted, I would get on the Zamboni and cut the ice before locking the doors and heading home. I'd get home about 1am, shower and fall into bed, awaken mid-morning, apply for jobs and then examine videos or make changes to the programming. As time went by, I applied for more and more jobs, and the jobs I applied for became less and less related to my skill set. They became based further and further away as desperation rose and my finances dipped. It was a peculiar situation to be in. I effectively had a full-time job programming and training the suit but my bank balance was going down week after week, and so I was getting less and less discerning with the jobs I was applying for. And I was really only doing a half assed job when actually applying for them. I treated it like a bulk exercise in ticking boxes. "Apply for twenty jobs a day." Tick. "Have lunch." Tick. "Laundry." Tick. "Programming." Tick. "Training." Tick.

Don't get me wrong. Every nibble I got, I pursued. Every coding test I received, I nailed. Every interview I managed to arrange, I sat in the office or on the Zoom call and intently nodded and sought to persuade the people on the other side that my biggest weakness was that I worked too hard, that I thrived in an ambiguous environment where priorities changed often, that I was both a self-starter and a team player, and that my five-year plan was to sit where they were now. But nothing. And so I quelled the growing panic as my redundancy pay dwindled and I worked on my passion project of getting my suit good enough to play in the professional leagues of ice hockey.

Although the suit was supposed to be effectively self-propelling and self-supporting, I still felt the sore muscles of a vigorous workout each morning after the session the night before. On top of that were all the bruises from the impacts with ice, boards and glass. But all that pain was just a badge showing me the progress that I was making. And, oh boy, the thrill I felt when I started on the puck handling and shooting! The feeling of skating fast around the rink… if I'd had hair it would have been flowing behind me. It felt like flying. Accelerating felt like being strapped to a rocket. Coming around the net and hitting my top speed after a series of crossovers and then doing it again with the puck only occasionally spilling from control was intoxicating. A few tweaks later and it was like the puck was on a string. My hands kept the puck in just the right position so then it was never underfoot and was always exactly where I needed it. My legs were always moving and there was no wasted movement, no times where the edges didn't grip just right, no parts where there was a wobble from bad balance. My head was a third system, looking around the rink at its own pace, deciding where to go and when to shoot, and where. Loading up for a slapshot did not result in me falling over 50% of the time. Graphing my slapshots wasn't a scatter plot anymore. I could and did pick my corners or ring the shot off the bar and then even pick up the rebound. My favorite move was to come down the middle of the ice, alternating between forwards and backwards with the puck gliding smoothly along with me and then hitting the blue line and smoothly letting rip a slap shot designed to hit the goal post and rebound straight back to me. Then I'd rock back on one heel to come to a halt with the puck on my back hand and roof it just under the crossbar. It was like a dance.

C. G. Lambert

It actually took me a little while to work out how to get that accuracy. One thing you never want to do was to look where you were going to shoot or pass the puck. The goalie and all other players would quickly realize what you were doing and you would be advertising the pass or shot and *boom*, the pass would be intercepted or the shot would be blocked. Making the suit read my intention could not rely on where I was looking. I ended up spending even more time examining the videos of professionals playing and mapping how they shot and how that could be mapped to my suit. Very basically, the shifts in where the player's body weight balanced on their skates before the shot could be determined from the video, and as long as I did something similar with my own body positioning, then the suit would know where I was aiming. Examining the posture and body positioning of players when they decided to pass instead of shoot, or more importantly when they kept hold of the puck instead of shooting, well, those were easy to program.

As I finished cutting the ice for the night, I wondered if I should ask for help from Seb or someone else from my team. I had gotten so much done already by myself that it just seemed to be a matter of pride that I didn't need anyone else's help. Looking back on it now, I realize that's an attitude that I had always had while programming and in that area, it was an ethos supported by that profession. Ice hockey was a team sport though.

The following evening, I made sure to catch up with Andrew. "So, tell me again what happens if the suit breaks?"

He blinked in surprise. "Well, I'm not going anywhere, so I can fix that for you. But if you are worried, I'll send you the blueprint. All you need is a 3D printer which can do metal and resin. It'll take a little while but it'll make a replacement square. To blend it back in just takes a few of those really small screwdrivers and you sort of lever it into place. I'll swap out a square and record it on video, just in case I'm not here and you need a quick fix."

"You're sure that using the suit doesn't use any of my own muscles? Because I've been aching since I've been using it - a good ache, like after the gym."

He paused for a second. "Maybe... maybe I was wrong. I mean, it is you doing the moving, right? The suit just magnifies and refines the motion. It's still you jumping and skating and such."

"If it's not muscle fatigue, could it be radiation?"

He laughed before seeing that I was serious. "Oh, no. There's no radioactive materials used, so you're not going to get cancer from the suit. There are electromagnetic fields involved but not even as strong as those on a trackpad for a laptop or the screen of your tablet or phone, so you're fine there too."

"So I'm just sore because I'm exercising?"

He shrugged. "I guess so."

The Practice

The thought of playing professional ice hockey was always front and center. It drove me relentlessly to improve the suit and to work through any and all obstacles in my way. But the more I succeeded in getting the suit to perform at the highest level, the more my off hours were spent thinking about what happened when and if I ever got onto the ice as a professional. I very quickly concluded that I would have to hide my past as much as possible. Because if anyone connected the professional player with all of their skill and abilities with the schlub playing beer league hockey, the only explanation for the sudden and absolute improvement would be something dishonest. Once there was a 'before' and an 'after', people would start looking for the reason for the difference. Then I would be in trouble. But if nobody knew what I was like now, then there would be no 'before and after', and I could point to my professional skills and claim somehow that I had always been this good. I'd just been off the ice for a while. I'd have to come up with a better story than that, obviously.

That was focusing on making sure there was no connection between the good player and my current ability. I would have to make sure the opposite was also true: that nobody seeing me now could connect me to the future professional. If word got out that I had a suit which allowed me to play ice hockey better than anyone else in the area, then there would be an easily discovered connection between me and the reason for my newly found expertise. If I ever wanted to play professionally, I would be found out faster than a paparazzi upskirt photo of the latest starlet getting out of a car. So the one thing I couldn't do was play in a league under my own name while fine tuning the programming of the suit. In fact, I would never be able to play with the suit as Phil Collins.

Ice time is expensive, so there are usually two teams on the ice for practices. Typically they take half the ice each and if they're not too far from each other in skill level, they might have a scrimmage at the end of the practice. I could never let anyone see me in the suit at my home rink. But there was another rink half an hour from me by Uber ride, so I researched which teams played and practiced over there. I ruled out the beer league teams as they might have people that I had or would one day play against. I needed a team or teams who played in a checking league, and I would also get no value from playing against young kids or first timers. That really narrowed down the teams, though I did note that the local high school used that particular rink.

I got a phone number for the coach of one of the youth league teams. They had a late-night session which usually meant that cost was a consideration. There were only so many early evening sessions and they usually had a premium attached, so anyone practicing at 11pm usually had one eye on the bill.

"Hey Coach Williams, my name is Peter Collins. I'm just returning to the country and want to get back on the ice and was wondering if I could join your team on Tuesday for your practice."

There was a pause as he considered this. The pause extended a bit far, so I thought I'd have to add something to allay any concerns he might be having. "I can pay for my share of the ice time of course and I'll get changed in the referee's changing rooms. I used to be quite good and I just want to see if I can shake the rust off."

"The boys play in the checking league, and they can get quite enthusiastic," the coach cautioned.

I was kind of hoping that would be the case. "Yeah, that's fine. I used to play at a high level, so I can handle that."

"Just out of curiosity, what level did you play at?"

I had no idea how to answer that question. Did I claim that I played professionally or just a high youth level? "Oh, the league no longer exists but it was at college."

"Awesome! We're having trouble making the ice payments so even one extra body will make a difference. See you Tuesday."

The 'referee's changing room' was a misnomer. It was just the first aid room on the pro-shop side of the rink, far from the bleachers with the changing rooms and showers underneath the seats. I arrived half an hour early and asked the rink manager for the key. He hesitated but I told him that I wasn't going to get changed with a whole bunch of high school kids because that's how rumors get started. He shrugged and told me to get it back to him at the end of the night. It was going to be a late night for him.

I got changed and then came out and introduced myself to Coach Williams. My helmet had a full cage from the times I used to wear glasses before the Lasik, and I noticed that all the players on the bench were also wearing full cages. Good - it would make it harder for anyone to recognize me.

I jumped onto the ice and did a few warm-up laps. God, it felt good to skate so easily. There were one or two among the kids who were tall, obviously the ones with their first growth spurts, but they were still a few inches shorter than me. They were all whippet thin though, so I certainly stood out. Heads swiveled to track me. I found a corner and started on a few stretches, and one of the boys came over to say hi. He immediately wanted to know who I was.

"I'm just sitting in for the session." He gave me a side eye but seemed to accept the explanation.

After warming up, we took a few shots on the goalie, keeping the puck low. I put about 50% into my wrist shots but they still zipped through the air and drew appreciative glances from the other players. A couple of the kids unleashed their slapshots which was a no-no in the teams I had played in. You don't want to hurt your goalie when they're just getting warmed up.

We went through some skating routines, with groups of three skating around each of the face off circles in turn. The first one forwards, then backwards, clockwise first and then anti-clockwise. I kept pace in my group, concentrating on keeping my edge work clean and well balanced.

Then we did some passing drills. I forgot how strong I had set up the suit, what with everything set to pro levels. My passes were blowing their sticks out of their hands. The coach stopped the drill, everyone grabbed a knee and he told them that a pass was a shot to a stick and that they had to be better at receiving the pass. Then he went through how to cradle the puck as it arrived, reaching out and slowing it down. He got me up to demonstrate both giving and receiving, and then we went back out and did it some more.

Finally we did a few breakouts, just repeating a very simple one. Dump the puck into the corner, the defenseman retrieves, passes to one of the wingers on the hash marks on the wall and then the winger hits the centreman skating up and out the middle. Then you go to center ice and the next group goes. We did that twice and the kids were performing well.

Then they added some complexity that took me an embarrassingly long time to figure out. In beer league, the focus is on getting enough players on the ice to have fun, and some players haven't been playing long, so their depth of hockey knowledge is limited to what they see on TV. The guys on the ice with me now may have been young but they had been playing for most of their lives, and their knowledge of drills was a lot more advanced than mine. So when the coach yelled out instructions about what F2 and F3 should be doing, it took me far too long to figure out what that meant and where I should be on the ice.

Then they added forecheckers. This was the first opportunity for throwing body checks that my fellow session attendees had, and they certainly wanted to let me know that they didn't appreciate being shown up in the passing drills.

I went into the corner to retrieve the puck and the forechecker came zooming in after me. I was going at maybe 30% pace and so I had maybe a second to realize that he wasn't letting up and would be putting me in the wall. I got rid of the puck and received the check cleanly with the suit doing a stellar job of absorbing the impact. It kind of looked like I just brushed him off. But he knew he had come in fast and that I should have been plastered against the glass. He skated away, shaking his head.

After that, the checks came faster and harder. I took it upon myself to use my speed to dodge them when I could and to take the hit to make the play when I needed to without getting the speed up over about 40%.

The kids took that as open season, like when your nephews are playing with you and realize that they can't hurt you, so the intensity of the play increases. I noticed the difference in enthusiasm between when I was the one in the corner or along the boards receiving the checks and when it was just them doing it to their own teammates. I smiled ruefully at the extra 20-30% effort they were giving it when I was on the receiving end.

I was worried about the kids noticing the effect that the suit was having on absorbing the impacts, so that was why I was using my feet to get out of the way. It was also great practice for keeping alert and knowing where everyone was on the ice.

The coach seemed to really like that exercise because we stayed doing breakouts for a bit longer than I would have in my own practices but eventually I noticed he had gone over to talk to the other coach. We made our way to the benches to have a scrimmage.

Coach Williams came by and assigned the lines. I was with two of the better players on the team and I finally took notice of the other team that had been practicing at the other end of the ice. They looked a bit older than my team, and seemed maybe a level higher. It made the scrimmage a little one sided, with the exception of when my line was on the ice.

They would set up in our defensive zone and cycle the puck very nicely, keeping possession and rotating through each of the forwards in the corner before eventually getting the puck out to the point man for a shot. With the three forwards in deep, there was always a screen and someone there to pick up the loose change. The problem with my team was that one-on-one, the players weren't able to mark their opponents close enough. Just a different level of speed and strength. That probably added to the frustration the guys felt during the drills. It was a different story when my line was on the ice though. We would leap over and I would usually close down their puck carrier, either stripping him of the puck or making him make a panicked pass or turn the puck over. Then we would be the ones on the attack, with a zone entry and then a simple cross ice pass and shot attempt. I would be the trailer, reclaiming the puck should we lose possession.

I kept clear of shooting mainly because the accuracy would be notable even if I was able to keep the shot speed low. I didn't want to attract too much attention but I did want to encourage contact. So it was balancing keeping the puck long enough for the opposition to target me with a good body check at the desirable end of behavior but steering clear of being a puck hog at the other end of the scale. I'd seen that elsewhere, where the guy that fancies himself hangs onto the puck doing impressive turns and spins while maintaining control of the puck, but never looking to pass or shoot themselves; just using it as an ego exercise to see how skilled they were. Inevitably in game situations, they would lose the puck at just the wrong second and the other team would end up with an odd man rush the other way.

So with me, I made sure I hung on for long enough to attract the body check and then got a pass away to the others. If my linemates bobbled the pass or lost it, I'd swoop in and get the puck back and then slow down near the boards, and maybe make a show of looking for the puck at my feet. No player in a checking league could pass up the opportunity to drop a big guy like me and by advertising that my head was down, they would be sure that I could not see them coming. Everybody likes bringing the big guy down. In the pro leagues, you can do what's called a reverse hit. That's when you are carrying the puck and you see the check coming and instead of just setting yourself up to receive it passively, you aggressively push back and initiate contact yourself. There was no way I would do that to these guys - they would be flung across the ice. Just before I received the check, I made sure that I would be able to do the reverse check if we'd been playing for keeps. But then I would get rid of the puck. The scrimmage was for the whole team to practice what they had learned doing the drills. Not for the ringer to stroke his ego.

When we came off the ice the first time, the center on my line looked over at one of our teammates on the bench. "Hey Jonesy, get used to the plus minus!"

I tapped him on the knee to get his attention and bent my head so then only he could hear me. "Don't mock your own teammates, man. Him feeling bad can only hurt the team." I caught his eye to make sure he was listening and he slowly nodded. "Now, we all know I'm going to get the puck. I need to hear you calling for the pass. I need to know where you want it. In deep, in the corner, in the slot, wherever you're going. And here's the thing. After you call, but before I pass it to you, have a look for where your other winger is. When you have the puck, it is too late to figure out what you are going to do with it, so figure that out before it gets to you. Can you do that?"

"Got it," he assured me, turning to the other winger on his other side and discussing what they would do next shift.

When we jumped over the boards the next time, they actually followed through. I got the puck, hit the hash marks against the wall and took the hit from the defenseman. I heard the center call for it in deep, and chipped the puck along the boards to where he could pick it up. I didn't see him look for the other winger but he must have known exactly where he was because he pulled off a lovely no-look pass and hit him in the slot for a beautiful one timer. It didn't go in but it was a lovely move and the tic-tac-toe of the passes made our whole line look good. The coach came by with pats on the backs for the other two guys after we got back to the bench.

Before too long, it was over and I thanked Coach Williams.

"Any time you want to share the ice time, let me know," he said as I paid him my share. "I think the boys enjoyed having you out there." I smiled and thanked him and headed back to the medical room and got changed.

When I came out and locked the door, the rink manager had just finished cutting the ice and was shoveling the ice from the Zamboni out the side door. I gave him the key to my private changing room and, feeling chuffed with myself, I headed to the door. One of the parents of one of the players cornered me on the way out. "Hey man, what's the story? You looked pretty good out there."

I mumbled something about having just returned from overseas and wanting to get back on the ice. He didn't buy it. "So, are you a professional or retired? Are you a scout?"

I shook my head as I headed out to the road and ordered my Uber for the return trip home. I would have to figure out a way of avoiding parents if I was going to use non-adult leagues to practice in. But I should have lots of great data to look back over when I got back home. Or maybe in the morning. The constant late nights were making me feel like a vampire.

The Agent

There are a hundred different types of ice hockey players. There are the intense 'win at all costs' types, then there are the friendly folk, and the quiet guys in the corner who don't say anything. All sorts. Beer league players tended to be on the more sociable end of the scale and they were helpful. Mainly. So, when I asked around for anyone who could steer me towards an agent, I eventually got in touch with a friend of a friend called Sonny Albright. He had played hockey at a high level and knew a few agents, so we'd arranged to grab a drink at a local sports bar.

"Hey, thanks for meeting with me. Much appreciated!"

"No problem, though I'm not sure what you're after."

"It's more of a thought exercise. A what-if scenario."

"Okay?"

"What if there was a really good player who wanted to play ice hockey professionally."

"As an adult or a kid?"

"An adult."

"Ah, easy. Any NHL team can sign them as an Unrestricted Free Agent so long as they're over 20."

"But how would you get an NHL team to want to sign them?"

"If they're playing college hockey, a scout will usually notice them in one of their games if they're as good as you say they are."

"Let's say that they're not playing college hockey."

Sonny frowned. "They're an adult, they're not playing college hockey, they're not playing professional hockey, and they're really good? How good are they? Because unless they've been playing overseas then... even then, there are scouts everywhere. I don't understand."

"Let's say that they are the best anyone has seen, better than Crosby, better than Ovi, better than McDavid or Beddard or Laffeniere. But they haven't been playing any organized hockey in a recognized league."

"Then how do you know that they are that good? If I got on the ice with a beginners' Learn to Skate class, I would look pretty good, right? You can only judge someone by the quality of the competition."

I stroked my chin. I had decided to omit a few attributes of this hypothetical really good player like his age and his pot belly. But I wanted to learn how I would be able to make it to the NHL.

"Let's say this player was a professional athlete in a different country where ice hockey wasn't known or was just a fringe sport."

"Okay."

"And so they hadn't played. But then they found out about it and jumped on the ice and they were a natural. Great balance, good strength, awesome endurance—"

"From being a professional in another sport?"

"Yeah. They spent a year learning the game and playing and working hard. What happens then? How do they get into the NHL?"

Sonny took a big swig from his beer. "Okay, got it. The normal way is that this player would have to attract the attention of an NHL team's scout who flags them as being a player to watch. Then a bunch of other scouts for that team all watch them play. Again, they're comparing the player with the rest of the players in their competition, and then comparing that competition with the level of the NHL. So this player needs to be playing in the most competitive environment possible - proper game situations where the games matter. Then if all the scouts from a team agree that this player is something special, they go back to the management team and tell them that they need to take a look at the player." Another swig of beer. "Alternatively, there are open tryouts at ECHL and AHL levels."

That sounded perfect! "Open tryouts? Like a pickup game or an open scrimmage?"

He snorted. "Don't let the name fool you. Your player would still have to submit a hockey resume and some video to justify their spot. It's not like an open cattle call. Nobody wants their time wasted."

"Right. That resume or video would again be against some recognizable level of opposition, right?"

"Yup."

I contemplated my beer for a bit. Sonny filled the silence.

"Unless this player got invited to a training camp with a PTO."

"A what now?"

"A Professional Tryout. Sometimes at the beginning of the season, there are NHL players who don't have a contract. Their previous team doesn't have a spot for them because they don't play the style that they're going for. So they get invited to a training camp to see if they're good enough and that training camp includes a bunch of pre-season games in September. The PTO is usually a favor that the GM owes an agent but occasionally the player will get a full-time contract and make the team. As I say, they're usually NHL players who have some sort of pedigree, not no-name randos, but I guess if this mystical player is as good as you say they are and they have an agent who has the ear of the GM, that would be another way for the player to get in front of the decision-makers in the NHL team."

"Oooh, that might work. So now all I need is an agent with the ear of a GM."

Sonny looked at me over his beer. "Look. Your typical agent probably gets like a hundred parents emailing them to say that they just have to come and look at their little Johnny because they are going to be the next Connor McDavid or Wayne Gretzky. There is a lot of money at stake. And of course, the parents just want what's best for their kid. So these agents are getting barraged with emails and phone calls."

"Even if they're not very good?"

Sonny frowned and leaned back. "Look, Mummy and Daddy are not the most objective of judges. All they see is the best in their kids. Plus they know that having an agent will be good for the kid, and they want bragging rights."

"But surely the fact that the player is an adult will work in their favor? No annoying parents to hassle them."

Sonny shook his head. "Did you hear about the guy who snuck into an NHL practice that was open to members of the public and got changed into his gear? He tried to do some drills with the team. This is the NHL team with a total salary north of what, $90M? This clown jumps the boards and goes one-on-one with the goalie. He figures the coach will see him on the ice and be so blown away that he will sign him immediately. But if he blows a tire going one-on-one with the goalie and barrels into him, he could rupture the goalie's MCL and then your number one goalie is out for the season just because there's a dude with an exaggerated view of his abilities."

"So this player I'm talking about, he's like your interloper, is he?" I enquired.

"Could be, maybe. Or maybe you're right and he's the real deal. But here's the thing. In real life, the number of people who actually have the ability that they think they have is very low indeed. The only people who can see the difference between how good you think you are, and how good you actually are, are the people who have performed at that level. That's why NHL coaches and scouts tend to be ex-NHL players. Usually. So if this player with no pedigree, and nobody vouching for them, gets anywhere near someone on the staff of an NHL team, they will think one thing - nutcase. So that's your first hurdle. I'll tell you what I'll do. I'll introduce you to an agent that I know and we'll pretend that you're a reporter doing a story on how players get signed and then you can feel them out in terms of how they might approach such a proposition. How's that?"

"That," I said, finishing my beer, "sounds like a plan!"

"So, Sonny tells me you're a reporter?" Patrick the agent and I were sitting in a booth in a bar downtown on the edge of the city. Patrick was a nugget of man, maybe fifty years old with the physique of a builder: strength with a purpose, not grown in a gym. He wasn't overly tall but his hand positively dwarfed mine and he exuded a no-nonsense attitude. It was a Tuesday, so the only customers were a pair of old guys who looked like they came as a set with the barstools. The barman was absently drying a glass while watching a game on a TV facing him on the wall.

"Let's just say I have a hypothetical that I want to run past you. What would be the oldest client you would take on?" I started.

He paused, moving the salt shaker around the table, staring at it the whole time. Eventually, he stopped. "What do you know about being an agent?" he asked instead.

I blinked. "Uh... you represent athletes and negotiate contracts for them?"

He nodded. "Sure, we do that. Amongst a whole bunch of other things but yes, we negotiate contracts. Do you know how we get paid?"

I was much more sure about this. "You take a percentage of the contract you negotiate."

"Bingo. Like any other representative, we take a cut: 3% or 5% if we're doing your taxes as well. If there's a team interested in the services of one of my players, and they're willing to pay for that service, whether it's the NHL, the AHL, the ECHL, a European league or anyone else, it really doesn't matter if the player is forty, fifty or sixty. If the team wants the player and they're willing to pay, then we will come to an arrangement and we'll take our commission."

I blinked. "Seriously?"

Patrick smiled. "We're the ultimate equal opportunity enabler. We don't care about gender, race, age or ability. All we care about is making the connection between a team wanting a player and the player wanting to play for that team."

"That's... that's awesome," I managed.

He was looking at me with a wry expression. "You look like you have a vested interest in that answer."

I was a little embarrassed that he'd seen through me so quickly. "Well… I'm relieved that age is no barrier."

"It certainly isn't… so is it someone you know?"

I couldn't progress without telling him it was me. But I hesitated because I didn't want to be seen as a nutcase. "It's me."

"Well, thanks for the drink, best of luck," he said as he stood up.

"Wait, wait. I know how it looks. But I'm telling the truth. I can play. Look, put me to the test. Put me in any situation with someone whose opinion you trust. Put me in a scrimmage with one of your players - it's the off-season, right?"

He didn't sit but did pause for a second, watching me. "Tell you what. Some of my players are playing in a summer league and I'll ask them to slot you in for a scrimmage or a game. I'll get somebody to make a video of it and then we'll have something to shop around if you're as good as you say. But if you're not, they'll tell you to get off the ice and you get off the ice. Once you get off the ice, you lose my number. How does that sound?"

"Sounds like a plan," I told him as I stood up and shook his hand.

The Deal

Patrick's office was in a high rise overlooking the city and he shared the floor with a law firm. If it was on a higher floor, it would have been a grand view but as it was, the neighboring building's reflective windows allowed me to see the outside of the building I was in, with the beautiful blue sky behind it. The secretary sent me in straight away and Patrick looked up from his desk with a smile and shook my hand. The office was compact but comfortable, a floor to ceiling bookshelf behind his desk light on books but heavy on photos of him with players, some posing mid-signing contracts. In a corner close to the window sat a circular coffee table between two low slung couches, but after a quick handshake, he beckoned for me to sit in the visitor chair at the desk.

Once I'd settled into the seat he leaned back and watched me with a raised eyebrow. "So, I've watched the tapes you sent through, and I've talked to Harry and Josh about how you went in their summer league and we might be interested in representing you. There are a few options and time is against us but there is a chance."

"That's great, thanks for that."

"I don't want you to get your hopes up. We'll only get one shot at this - we're too close to the start of training camps so we can really only choose one. Our best bet is with one of the teams who are rebuilding. They'll have the most incentive to get to the cap floor and so will be ready and able to take a risk on you."

"Oh… I was kind of hoping to play for my favorite team."

He grinned. "Well, that's certainly something we can try. Luckily for you, I have a very good relationship with their GM. He's going to want to have the details of the contract worked out before you turn up though."

I frowned. "Why would he want to do that?"

"Mainly so that you don't think that you're going to get a $15M deal. It's to set your expectations. But it's also to lock you into playing for his team. Let's say you're as good as you say you are and he's sitting on the bargain of the century. There's nothing to stop the GM of his arch-rival team to hear about you and offer more money. The rival GM has the benefit of you having gone through the training camp and having proven that you can play in the league. He has the cap space to offer you more money. So the GM of your favorite team will want to lock you in."

"I'm not going to make $15M?"

"Not in year one. Look, I'll tell you how the negotiations are going to go. I'm going to go to him and tell him that you can walk on water and that you can outskate, outhit, and outdeke anyone on his roster. But nobody will pay you $15m in your first year. At forty, you're too old. You'll get league minimum - $775k. On top of that, they're going to want a two-way deal with $80k in the minors. Because as much as they trust me when I tell them that you are Gretzky, Mario and Steven all rolled into one, he needs to be able to have a risk-free way to get you off the roster if it turns out that I'm wrong."

I frowned as I tried to figure out which Steven he was referring to. Stamkos? Yzerman?

"We've reduced his risk to the same as dealing with any player. He'll have to send one of his waiver-exempt players into the AHL to make space for you but if the upside is as promised, that's an easy decision. Now that his risk is taken care of, what about your reward? $775k is the league minimum. I won't be able to get more than that but what I can do is get you some incentives. Let's say, $50k if you play 20 games, $100k if you play 40 games and another

$100k if you play 60 games. Now I know that he's pretty close to the cap ceiling, so that's what I should be able to get going into the training camp. But if you knock their socks off, that's not the deal we'll be signing."

My smile froze. The dollar signs in my eyes dropped away. "No?"

"No. If he's getting a $15M player, but paying less than $1M then there's no way that's fair and it is going to leave a very bad taste in your mouth. He will want you playing happily, not reluctantly. So the day after training camp finishes, we'll sit down over a desk and we'll say, 'Let's bump that bonus up so that if you make it to 20 games that you actually make $1M."

"And the other bonuses too?"

He frowned and got to his feet, prowling close to the window before continuing. "Probably not. You see, the contract without the bonuses will put the team against the cap. Any bonuses will put them over the cap, so those will have to come out of the following year's cap. So $250k will be easier to swallow. It's nothing, and $1.5M will not be nothing. I know that it's still a bargain, right? A $15M+ player for $2.25M. But here's the silver lining. In year two, and for as long as you're playing at the highest level, you can command market price because they will find a way to make that work. You would have proven to them that you can play with the big boys."

Now it was my turn to frown as I considered the situation, swiveling in my chair to face him at the window. "But won't they screw up their team structure doing that? I've seen those Tetris charts with all the players and their salaries and how many years they have left on each of their contracts."

"What, getting the best player in the league for zero draft picks? Any GM would take that deal. You're worried about the players they would have to move? Let's say that you play as well as you say you can. Come January 1st, the GM is going to ring me and ask if you are interested in playing the next season and can we negotiate an extension. I'll say yes, and we'll agree on a number with a fantastic number of zeros in it. It'll be a one-year extension. You'll get a huge chunk of it as a signing bonus because you have leverage and it won't matter to the team. I'll let you and the tax authorities fight over whether that gets taxed as income or as a bonus. It all counts towards the cap. We'll sign that extension, and you'll get a press conference, and you'll say it's great to have a commitment and a home for the next year and a half. The team will say that they're glad to lock in someone of your caliber and abilities, and you'll all smile for the camera." He took a breath and grinned.

"Then the team will have until July to find a team to take the three or four players whose current salaries will add up to about $20M. That's your $15M for next season, the extra $1M from the bonuses this year which won't fit under this year's cap, plus the salary of the four players who will replace them. The GM doesn't have to pull the trigger on those trades just yet. He can wait until any time before the next season starts. Sure, he has to find players to replace those he's traded away. But again, he has time to do that. He can get draft choices coming back the other way in exchange for the players that he's losing which are always helpful. But I'll tell you something, those cheaper replacement players will be on one-year contracts."

"Why is that?"

"Because let's say that you retire, get hurt, or decide to become a surfer dude after year two. Your salary comes off the books because you're not playing. If those new, cheaper players are on long-term contracts, then their admittedly low salaries stick around. Which is not advisable, because for the team to go back to how it was before you showed up, they would need to find players like they had originally - those three or four players earning $20M. But the GM won't mind that task because that's what they are doing every year. Trying to find bargains. With talent like yourself, that's almost impossible because there are fewer players as good as you, and those players have choices." He made a pyramid with his hands. "The rookies and the players a year or two off retirement at $1M, the regulars at $3M, the veterans at $6M plus and the star players getting $10M or more. As you go up the pyramid, the number of players at that level decreases. So the lower the price point, the easier it is to find replacements. Does that all make sense?" He returned to his spot behind his desk as he waited for my response.

"I guess so. I just thought I might get more money because I'm so good."

"Yeah, you're good but it's a business decision. It's all about risk and how defensible a decision is to the boss."

"What, the GM?"

"No, no. The GM reports to the president or the owner. So, if the GM announces that they've signed someone who is your age and has zero history in any professional league, and they pay you $15M and move players out of the team to make way for your salary, then the owner is going to look at the GM and wonder what he is smoking. I guarantee the GM making that deal will get fired and the first thing his replacement will do will be to dump you and try to get back to how the roster looked like before Mr. Peter Collins showed up. But, if he's only paying league minimum and not having to lose any fan favorites to slot you into the starting lineup, then the conversation changes. It's not that the GM is betting everything on you. He's now making an educated bet with the same level of exposure as he would make with any player, just with an enormous upside"

"Okay, so how much will I get paid?"

"During the regular season, you will get your salary paid every two weeks for six months. So you'll get $60k gross - call it $30k in the hand. But save a lot of that because you don't get anything after the regular season. If you get sent down to the minors, you'll be on a tenth of that, and don't buy a place to live too soon. The last thing you want is to find yourself with a mortgage on a place near the NHL team. When you get sent down and play in the AHL team, you need to find a place near where the AHL team plays as well, and you'll only be getting paid your AHL salary. That's a recipe for disaster."

"So the first payment is…"

"Mid-October."

My face dropped. With the cost of getting to the summer league and paying for the hotel and food while I was there, my bank balance was not looking healthy at all.

"Don't worry. The team will fly you to them, they'll put you up in a hotel for the Training Camp, you'll get $500 per game you play and they'll pay you a per diem. A per diem is walking around money. Per diem means each day. Whenever you're away from home, you get it. So as long as you can make it through the cuts at Training Camp, the ball is in your court. I'll give you a call after I've had a chat with the GM. Fingers crossed!"

After I left his office, I stopped off at the local branch of my bank and used the ATM to empty my account. From now on, I didn't want anything to connect me to my previous life. I'd pay cash for everything, and I would be reverting to the name on my birth certificate. Kind of like going off the grid. Maybe I should shave...

Before Training Camp

A series of emails from the player liaison office later, and I was directed to a hotel near the practice facility where I would stay for the two-week-long camp. There were so many of us staying at the hotel that the team put on a bus, even though it was less than half a mile between the hotel and the training facility.

The email briefing was comprehensive. It covered the times the bus would pick up and drop off at the hotel, who was in which squad and an itinerary. I noticed that the itinerary only covered the time until noon and when I asked my agent about this, he said that contractually, the team could only have you for three hours each day.

The players were split into four squads, each with a slimmed down roster of a goalie, four defensemen and six forwards. The players were all under contract to the team but depending on their age and quality, they played in a wide range of leagues. So some were in the NHL, some were in feeder teams in the AHL or ECHL and some were playing in professional leagues in Europe.

In the documentation attached to the email, they had the player profiles, with photos, ages, heights and weights, which league the player had most recently played in and a "hockey CV" of notable events during their career. Trophies and awards won, that sort of thing. Buried in that player data was me, with the letters PTO beside my name and very little else. It looked like the printer had run out of ink on that page, there was so little data about me. I also noticed that there were three other players that were also on PTOs.

I was surprised when my agent had told me that in addition to the per diem of $50, I would be also getting $500 per game of "contract income" while I was in camp. The thing to remember, he went to great pains to tell me, was that I could be cut at any time and that would stop the free food, hotel room, and payments. While it wasn't likely that I would be cut during the first few days of training camp, it was always possible. It would be more likely I would be one of those let go in the daily cuts in the second half of camp as they let players head back to their overseas team or back to their AHL team, or in the case of those on PTOs, back to obscurity or retirement. If I could make it through each of those culls, then I might make it to the preseason games. And if I lived up to my hype and got the coach and management on side, then I might expect a professional contract to be offered through my agent. No pressure.

If I had been younger, I might've been more stressed by the pressure. The rookies in camp had been playing top level age group hockey for ten or fifteen years, all with the goal of making it to this two-week camp. I guessed that they had learned some way of handling that mental strain during all those years of being the best in their year, at their school or in their team. Some way of feeling the pressure but performing to their best anyway. And while I didn't have those techniques, I also didn't really have all that much pressure. I wasn't dealing with any insecurities or uncertainty about whether I could perform at this level because I had built a suit programmed with the performance of the best players and then juiced slightly with an additional 5%. I might even turn it up some more should I find myself slipping behind.

However, I was beginning to realize that the one thing I hadn't programmed was my brain. The players around me had developed their physical abilities in tandem with their mental ones - their brain worked at the same speed as their body. Me? I was a 10mph brain in a 100mph body. So I was very aware that I would have to try and think fast and address that difference as a matter of some urgency.

The parting words of my agent had been "You need to dress smartly – there's a contractual dress code you have to adhere to," so I went out and bought a suit and a couple of shirts from the local department store. The labels on the suit definitely did not say Armani or Gucci. Once the money in my pocket ran out, I was done. If this didn't work out, I was really going to have to try and find some programming work in a hurry.

So I rocked up to the hotel with my department store suit in a suit bag over my shoulder, a gym bag with my patchwork hockey suit hidden under my gym gear and battered ice hockey skates and a wheelie bag with my casual clothes. It was sobering to see my whole life boiled down to what I could carry in both hands. Is this all I had to show for my forty years?

The camp didn't start until the following morning, the bus was scheduled to pick us up at a quarter to eight and there was an email reminding us to have a good breakfast beforehand. I checked in and received an envelope of cash from reception with my name on it. This was the per diems for the first few days.

I went to the room and it was a little on the smaller side, a single. After putting my clothes away, I took the opportunity to call my flatmates. I knew that Seb wouldn't answer his phone so I called him using a secure app.

"Hey Seb."

"Phil! Where are you?"

"I'm at training camp. I have a chance to make the pro team. How cool is that?"

"Hey man, that's awesome, well done. Hey, your little suit is getting some attention. Andrew has been talking to a Russian guy for the past hour and I can't understand a word they're saying. When will you be coming back?"

"I'm not sure, hopefully never if I make the team."

"So what do we do about your part of the rent? You're still on the lease you know?"

"Oh, yeah I completely forgot about that. Well, if I make the team, I'll be earning a lot of money, so that won't be a problem."

"Okay, well, as long as you're having fun and we're not out of pocket, then all good. Let us know though, yeah?"

"Sure, will do. I'll get my name off the lease if I do make the team, okay?" In the background, I could hear the raised voices of an argument getting out of hand.

"Cool. Gotta go - sounds like there's a little disagreement going on. Talk later, okay?"

"Sure, bye!"

I was at a loss for what to do with my afternoon and evening. I had already spent some time researching the sorts of exercises that were likely to be required at the training camp. I used the same video processing techniques that I had for the on-ice movements to generate the data that I would need for the off-ice tests. While I was getting the video footage, I also checked to see what was considered to be good performance. That had all gone into programming the suit with a different suite of motions and abilities. I saw the physical tests as necessary gates to navigate prior to getting on the ice. Once I was on the ice, then I would excel.

I watched some TV and then had dinner downstairs in the hotel restaurant. On the way back up in the lift, I bumped into Charlie Peckham, one of the veterans on the team. It was a little intimidating - he was maybe an inch shorter than me but had the classic chiseled features of an athlete. I nodded a greeting and he smiled and nodded back, maybe thinking that I was a fan rather than someone who would be on the ice tomorrow along with him.

Back in my room, I made the mistake of surfing the net and noticed that my presence in the training camp had proven story worthy. All of the stories started with a general run down of which position had the most questions around it, and which players from last year had the most to prove. And then they got to me.

'Mystery man,' 'enigma,' 'unknown,' were all mentioned. The press pack that the media had been given had the same player data that we'd received in the training camp welcome email. Mine was notable for a couple of reasons. The first was the weight. Those numbers were totally out of step with everyone else's. I wasn't the tallest but I was close. Most players who were tall were in the 220lbs to 240lbs area. Someone who was 6' 6" was expected to carry a bit more weight. But my 6' 4" height coupled with close to 300lbs stuck out to the journalists. They all commented on the fact that I had no history in terms of what was listed in the media guide or what they could find online. Where I really made my mistake was continuing reading into the public comments under the news stories.

There were the inevitable comments on the weight or age, but then someone had also added: *Every year I feel the need to remind everyone that the addition of players on tryouts are there to make up the NHL's need for a certain number of players with NHL experience for the preseason games.*

Someone responded to that, calling out the fact that I had no NHL experience, therefore I wasn't there for that reason. They answered that challenge: *I guess he's here on a Make a Wish sort of thing then.*

And that was one of the more generous toned conversations about me. I managed to tear myself away from the negativity online and got to bed early. The next step in my big adventure was only one sleep away.

***

I got up at six and had a shower, and then dressed and went down for breakfast. I was torn. My normal breakfast whenever confronted with a buffet would have been a plate of bacon, eggs, sausage, hash browns, a plate of fruit and a plate of pastries or waffles or pancakes if they had them. But what I felt that I should have as a professional athlete was maybe cereal, fruit and yogurt or an egg white omelet. I compromised... sort of. I had the egg white omelet... and then added bacon and the hash browns and went back for the waffles with honey and butter. I also had an orange juice and a coffee. I figured that I would be working off the calories, even if they could only have us for three hours.

After brushing my teeth and shaving, I contemplated what to wear. I needed to turn up wearing the newly bought suit but would I be okay carrying my special hockey suit with my gym gear or should I wear it under my clothes? I had worn the hockey suit for lengthy periods of time while trialing it at the ice rink and it kind of felt like a thin wetsuit - it hugged my body but wasn't restrictive or too tight, and it was a little thicker than lycra or gym clothes. I had to admit that towards the end of one of my marathon skating sessions, when I was sweaty and gross, I regretted not making some sort of vent that could wick the sweat away from my body.

I decided in the end to carry my hockey suit with my gym gear. I gave myself one last look in the mirror, took a deep breath and then headed down to the lobby to wait for the bus. While in the lobby, I watched the steady arrival of other players, some of them greeting each other familiarly in the case of the team regulars. The rookies and prospects weirdly didn't say hello to each other but instead had the familiarity borne of being around people you knew. I'd find out later that they had already spent a week together in the Rookies camp.

I watched, trying to keep a poker face on. I couldn't connect names to faces of any of the prospects or rookies but all of the first team regulars were very familiar. The only thing that threw me were the relative heights. When you're only used to seeing the players from their mugshots or TV interviews, you kind of assumed they were all the same height. I certainly wasn't going to go all fanboy and 'Squeeee!' But being around so many of the first team players all at once was the first indication that what was happening was for real.

At the appointed time, the bus turned up. I had to point out my name on the clipboard of the person checking us off, and when I got aboard, I saw one or two eyebrows being raised. Looking at the other players on the bus, I felt awkward about my appearance. These guys were either super slim and yet to grow into their bodies if they were the young guys, or else were solid specimens if they were regular first team players - either way, their suits looked tailored and fit the way that suits were supposed to fit. Rather than the way my suit sort of rumpled and flapped. Anyway, the bus didn't take long at all to get to the training facility and we filed out and headed upstairs to one of the meeting rooms. I hadn't realized just how many players there would be. There must have been sixty of us. We filled the seats in the meeting room and other coaching staff stood around the periphery.

There the coach greeted us and gave a little speech. He mentioned that the team had made good progress over the last year and that he was glad of the development everyone had made but that no roster slots were given and that everything was up for grabs. He mentioned that there were four of us there on PTOs and that at the end of the two weeks, he hoped that everybody had left everything on the ice because he wanted there to be no regrets. A few heads turned to look around when he mentioned the PTOs but after the brief chat, he pointed us to the changing rooms. I found a corner of the changing room and put on my suit and then my gym gear. And then the testing started.

Testing

We'd been divided into four squads and went through a very well drilled set of tests with the strength and training team. There were no do-overs. You'd give the person at the station your name. Then you'd do the test, they would write down the results and then the next person would step up.

I had no idea how much notice would be taken by the coaching staff of my performance: how much my possibly very short future with the team might be dictated by how fast I could run between markers or how high I could jump in the air. So I tried my hardest on each of them.

There was a vertical jump test. A timed sprint. How many pushups I could do. How many pull ups. How much weight I could squat on each leg, and then a couple of endurance tests which made some of the guys throw up afterwards. I had done my research and so I knew what times would be considered good and I made sure I placed there or thereabouts. I didn't want anyone getting suspicious by overachieving but by the same token, I didn't want to lose out before I even got into my skates.

We all went en masse into the changing rooms and there was a full set of gear waiting, hanging with a practice jersey with my name on the back. As we did a few laps of warm-up and then stretched, I looked around the edge of the rink. I had to stop myself from doing double takes. Once I had the right mindset, I could recognize probably a quarter of the people around the rink as alumni from previous year's teams. That wasn't just a scout or skills coach watching from the bleachers. That was a cup winner from the team's last heyday. That guy there had a thousand games in the league and more than half of those were in the team's colors. The inner fan within me wanted to go around with an autograph book and just talk to them all about their experiences. "Remember that time that you scored that goal in the final? Remember flattening that guy?" And they were going to be watching me try to put together a Cinderella story of rags to riches.

I had to focus on myself rather than who was watching, so I turned my gaze to the ice, stretching while boring a hole in the ice with my stare. I forced myself to concentrate on my breathing. I reminded myself I had the suit. I had tested and tested it. It was set up well. It would work. I just had to make sure I did my bit. No false starts. No falling, no slipping, no losing an edge and definitely no getting hurt. Or worse - hurting someone else. Could you imagine? A 40-year-old rookie goes to training camp and takes out the team's top three players in a sprinting accident. I laughed despite myself and one of the rookies glanced up from their own thoughts, shocked that someone was relaxed enough to laugh. "Keep loose kid," I told him with a big smile. My gallows humor focusing on the absolutely worst thing that could happen made me realize what an absolute privilege it was to be there, trying out for the team. From that moment on, I resolved that I would have fun and give it my all.

The first test was a sprint from the goal line to the far blue line. As they set us all up on the goal line, I noticed all the video cameras set up all over the place. There wasn't too much spacing with fifteen of us spanning the width of the ice. We all got into one version or another of our sprinting poses and then the whistle blew.

I took off the fastest I could and led the line of players by about a length, with the goalies following along a little further back. That felt good. The coaches gave us a few minutes to recover before assembling us at the halfway point and getting us into single file. This time, it would be one by one, starting at halfway, going around the net and then back to halfway. They had put us in the order we had finished the first sprint, and I looked around from my place at the front of the queue. The coach looked at me and raised an eyebrow. He had a whistle in his mouth and a stopwatch in his hand. Like an old school stopwatch, not a phone with a stopwatch app. I took a deep breath, got into my sprint pose and nodded. The whistle went and I took off. My feet were a blur, going from straight line sprinting take-off into power crossovers as I rounded the net and then into strong strides as I came out of the corner and into the neutral zone. I passed the coach at high speed and my momentum kept me going the length of the ice. I checked out who was in the crowd as I glided around the net at the other end of the ice. There was a lot of chatter and a fair few wide eyes as I returned to the end of the queue of players. I saw the coach skate over to someone on the side of the ice and talk briefly to them before he returned to the center of the ice and addressed the next skater. The person he had spoken to at ice edge took off running, leaving the rink. We went through about half the players by the time he returned followed by the GM. A little frisson rippled through the rink as the GM took up position near halfway. The players noticed that and I could see the focus and concentration levels jump from an already intense 105% up to a 120%. That intensity led to one of the players losing an edge as he rounded the net, resulting in him crashing into the boards. He picked himself up and finished the half lap and the coach declared that we'd go through again to make sure that they had a good time for each of us. He glanced at the GM as he said that, so I'm not sure I believed the reasoning but whatever.

I didn't know what my time had been but I knew that the GM had been called because it had been good, so all I had to do was to do something similar and the GM would have me categorized as a speedster. Which would have to be a good thing, right? A big guy who could move was hella rare - the additional height and higher mass made bigger guys slower even if the chance for a longer leg stride partly offset that. It was never a simple equation with ice hockey!

Anyway, I may have imagined it but when it was my turn again, there was a collective holding of breath from everybody in the rink as I took my mark. When the whistle blew, I took off again and this time I went a little wider around the net because by then the ice had had fifteen guys skating hard over the same parts and so was a bit cut up. The extra angle allowed me to push harder through the crossovers because the turn wasn't quite as tight and I came out puffing but happy with my speed and crossed the finish line with a lunge to show that I cared about the finish.

The Forty Year Old Rookie

I was bent over from the effort as I cruised around the other net at the far end of the ice and by the time I circled and came back to the players in the middle, I missed whatever interaction between coach and GM might have happened. There did seem to be an increase in the hubbub from the people watching and the players were staring at me as well. I wasn't used to being the center of attention for good reasons on the ice and so it was a novel feeling. I kicked myself internally - I should have prepared myself better psychologically. This whole plan was set up so that I would definitely be noticed and my normal state of trying to slip under the radar was not going to work now. Scrutiny would be a symptom of my success.

All the other players went through their second go and then we spread out again along the goal line. We'd tested for speed and now it was time for a couple of endurance tests. The first was sprinting from the goal line to center ice and back until failure. The whistle blew and we took off. As soon as I turned for my second lap, I could see that some players were going at less than 100%, maybe in an attempt to preserve their energy and go on for longer. I didn't care and kept going at top speed. I'd thought long and hard about this test and decided that I would need to reduce my pace to show that I was human and tiring but that I would stay at the front of the pack.

C. G. Lambert

I managed ten before I was a lap ahead of the others and players started dropping out at lap twelve. There were three or four who were still on the same lead lap that I was on but they were far behind me. I slowed down whenever someone dropped out and by the time I was the only one left I was making a great show of skating in pain and stopped soon after that. The performance seemed to have impressed the observers and a smattering of applause trickled across the ice. I went to the boards and got some water and sat on the bench, huffing and puffing, quite convincingly, I thought.

The coach gave us some more time to recuperate and then the final on ice test came up. Sixteen laps of the ice as fast as we could go. As he announced the test, he gave us a word of caution. It was a long way and he didn't want anyone pulling or tweaking anything.

And off we went. This time I was just interested in enjoying the skate and staying in front of everyone else, so I just skated at an enjoyable speed and whenever anyone passed me, I would get back in front. I made sure I passed quite wide to make sure I didn't bump them or otherwise interfere. At one point, I started passing the stragglers and by the end of the session, I skated easily and joined the gasping and bent over skaters as we made our way to the benches and the water. I thought the training staff were looking at me strangely but shrugged it off as paranoia. I later found out that I had actually done seventeen laps and had still broken the record for the best time.

We got off the ice and had our choice of the post-exercise facilities. There were ice baths, masseuses and sessions on the mats with foam rollers. I contemplated having a massage but the veterans were already queuing, and the ice baths were all taken by the regulars from the first team. I grabbed a foam roller and found a spot on the mat and followed the instructions of the training staff. A couple of the rookies were beside me and as we stretched, one of them spoke to his friend beside him. "I blew a tire in the sprint; I hope that doesn't count against me."

His friend noticed me listening and shook his head. "I don't think anyone will remember your blown tire," he said, obviously referring to my performance on the ice.

"You got around okay on your second go though, didn't you?" I asked him.

He seemed surprised that I was talking to him and nodded.

"So that should count okay." I told him. He seemed pleased, although whether that was due to me talking to him or what I had said, I wasn't sure.

His friend introduced himself. "I'm Thomas - I'm in the juniors. How do you skate like that?"

I was immediately aware that the rest of the gym was listening in. "I'm not sure, Thomas. I've read so many training books over the years, I'm not sure which ones have the best advice. So it's like all the guidance from all those books, plus a bunch of time in the gym."

Thomas nodded. "Cool, I'll work on it. Maybe by next year I'll have a bit more speed."

I looked at him. "Aren't you trying to make the first team this year?"

Thomas frowned. "From my league? No, that's not going to happen. I'm just glad to practice with real NHL players."

I looked around. The gym was filled with the rookies and those from the minor leagues. The older guys were all getting massages or were immersed neck deep in ice baths. "It's great that you have realistic expectations on what you might get out of camp."

"Yeah, it's more about letting the coaching staff see your progression since last camp and to show you what's required to get to the first team."

Eventually we finished our cool down and got changed and then it was onto the bus. We arrived at the hotel mid-afternoon and while on the way back, I could hear guys arranging to meet at the bar or in one of the rooms to play cards, grab a drink or just chill. Nobody extended an invite to me and I didn't want to be that guy on the edge of the groups looking expectant waiting for an invite, so I wandered through the lobby after everyone else had gone, not dawdling, just knowing that if I went up to my room alone I would end up watching TV or doom scrolling on the internet. I decided to prolong my journey to my room with a detour to the front desk.

"Uh, were there any messages for me? Collins, room 341."

The receptionist checked under the desk. While she was down there, my eyes wandered aimlessly along the reception desk and I spied a stack of newspapers. On the cover, there was a photo of a crater and debris from an explosion.

"Nothing, I'm afraid," the receptionist said as she stood back up.

"Can I take this?" I asked, pointing to the paper.

"Of course," she replied.

I wandered back to my room, slowly reading the front page. The caption had mentioned that the explosion had occurred in my suburb. The buildings that had survived the explosion looked very much like our neighbors' buildings.

Training Camp

When I got back to my room, I threw myself on the bed and devoured the story. They said that there had been a gas leak and that there had been three casualties, and they named me and my two flatmates. Well, 'Phil Collins' and my two flatmates. I couldn't believe it and tried getting in touch with them on their mobiles and any of the many social apps they both used. Nothing. I shook my head. Something didn't add up. First of all, the news reports seemed pretty adamant that the explosion was caused by a gas leak but the gas lines didn't go anywhere near our neighborhood - we were on electric. Second of all, there was no mention of a coroner's report or any dental records tested or anything, which would indicate that they knew for certain that it was me lying in the morgue. Lastly, the time of the explosion was very soon after the call that I'd had with Seb the previous night. I started shaking.

I got myself a drink of water and tried to calm down. It really looked like someone had blown up my flat, killing my flatmates.

That, and they thought I was dead. I tried to remove the emotion and think through the ramifications but all I could focus on was the loss of my two flatmates. I spent the next half an hour stalking up and down my room, crying. Real tough guy, right?

Once I pulled myself together a little, I tried to figure out who I should tell. There was a Fire Chief named in the story, so maybe that was the right person to talk to. Or the police if it was some sort of assassination. But then I paused. If someone had gone to the trouble of blowing up a suburban house to kill three people, what would they stop at if it turned out that their explosion had not been totally effective? Plus, unless any of my flatmates had talked to anyone else about the suit, then very conveniently, I was the only person left alive who knew about it. I mulled that over. The fact that there had been someone visiting Andrew made it less likely that I was the only one left alive who knew about the suit. Had he been trying to sell the technology to the Russians? Or was the accent just a coincidence? Were they a friend from his work who just happened to be Russian? I splashed some water over my face. This was a big deal.

I'm not proud of where my mind went next but after the emotional shock and grief went away, I selfishly thought about what would happen if I did not make the team. I would be heading back to the smoking remnants of my apartment with a few dollars in my pocket and no job, no clothes, no personal effects and just my laptop and my gym gear as my only possessions. If I needed any more motivation to make the team, this was it.

The next day, the bus picked us up again and we went into the facility. This time we would be doing on ice practices for an hour and then a whole lot of off-ice sessions - video sessions, diet sessions, systems sessions and such.

I was in the first group on the ice and it was... interesting. It would have been fun if so much wasn't riding on my performance. We did skating drills which I nailed and then we did passing drills, which I nailed again. We did shooting drills which I... you guessed it, nailed. It was like a test where you knew the answers - no, scratch that, it was like a test that you had just sat and had already had a chance to go away and find the answers to the questions that you didn't know. Then you got to sit the test again. Even the more complex drills went well. As I was a rookie, I went last and the other veterans in the squad all went first. This meant that I could see what I needed to do in the drill. All of the drills were a lot more complex than the simple things we did in beer league, so it took a couple of demonstrations before I knew what was going on. Even the younger guys picked it up quicker than I did but by the time it was my turn to do the drill, you would never have known. I was getting to the puck first, I was making crisp tape to tape passes and when it came to getting a shot on net, the goalie facing me might as well not have been there.

The coaching staff didn't seem to be watching me particularly but every now and then, I would catch a pair of staff, on ice or off, talking quietly while very obviously checking me out.

Afterwards, in the changing room, I took off my jersey and folded it and placed it carefully in my stall. Then I took off my pads and stood there for a second in what looked to everyone else like a patchwork wetsuit. It attracted a few glances and stares from my fellow players and the guy in my neighboring stall leaned over to feel the material. He blinked in surprise. "What's that?" he asked. I nodded. It may have looked like wetsuit material but it had more of a plasticky feel but still flexed. It had a patchwork effect as a result of being built of small square patches joined together and even though they were all supposed to be black, the resins and plastics that Andrew had used had all been subtly different, as he had explained. So even though anyone would have described the suit as black, it was really a hundred shades of black.

"It's an anti-slash suit," I told my neighbor. "It protects against cuts from skate blades and also protects against concussions."

"Oh, ok," he replied and went back to what he was doing.

That was easy. I peeled it off and one of the equipment guys came over and took it off me. I half-heartedly protested but didn't want to draw attention to it by making a fuss but I did follow him to the door of the room where he was putting it into a gear bag with my number on it.

"I'll take good care of it," he replied when he saw that I had followed him.

"It's really important to me. I don't know what I would do without it."

"I'll make sure it's well taken care of." He looked at it more closely. "It looks like you've had it for a long time."

I nodded. "There's a lot of memories there," I agreed.

"Well, it will be washed and ready to go for practice," he said, and then went back into the room for more gear.

"Uh, when you put it out, could you put it on its hangar behind my jersey? Just so nobody sees it, is all." I said, trying not to sound pitiful.

But all he did was nod and make a note on a clipboard and that was that.

The equipment guys did a great job of looking after the gear. They made sure that the pads and gloves were all aired and dried prior to the trainings and games, that they had spare gloves available during the game and they also made sure that each stall in the changing rooms had the gear nicely arranged with the jerseys on hangers.

Now, one of the things that the equipment guys were also responsible for is all of the superstitious nonsense that players believe with regards to any piece of equipment. They do that, not because they believe that if you align the elbow pads with the shin pads that you will have a better game, but because you might, and if they do those special requests, then the player will feel better about their game and may perform better. It's their job to make sure that the player feels as good as they can about their gear, so from their point of view, a request to take the suit away as soon as I shed it and make sure that it was hidden behind my jersey at practices and games was a very basic and simple task.

The off-ice nutritional sessions seemed to be pitched mainly at the younger guys and covered a pretty in-depth curriculum. I was surprised until the nutritionist taking the session mentioned that in the league's efforts to get even a sliver of an advantage, getting the fuel right for the engine of the athlete's performance made perfect sense. It was only a matter of time before there was a sleep specialist coming in to talk to the players.

There were two things that I was not expecting. One was the photo shoots that took place over the whole time I was at the training camp. A room had been set up with lights and backgrounds and periodically, one of the players would be tapped on the shoulder. He would disappear into the room and come back out twenty minutes later and get back to whatever we were doing. When it was my turn, it was just standing in front of a white screen with lights shining brightly, posing with a hockey stick. A couple of shots looking tough and a couple looking down the barrel of the camera. A variety of casual poses leaning on the stick or taping the butt of the stick, just photos of a player doing something player-related so then it didn't look weird. The photographer had to ask me twice if I was Peter Collins before he took my affirmation as fact. I guess the age and body shape were a bit confusing for him. I behaved myself and did the poses he asked for and then went back to the nutrition session.

The other thing I was really surprised by was the press. There were press guys in the practice sessions. They were interviewing players after the on-ice sessions and they bulked out the audience watching the on-ice sessions. They didn't have old-timey hats with a card saying 'Press' sticking out of the brim but they were the only ones in the stands not wearing a tracksuit or business suit, so their lack of uniform turned out to be a uniform in a way and made them easy to spot. I largely avoided them if I could, keeping my head down and resorting to ducking into meeting rooms to keep away from the more determined-looking of them. Which meant that I ended up asking a lot of the staff for notes and documentation to support the sessions that they had been running. I had to justify bursting into their rooms while trying to escape reporters, right?

And so by the time the bus came to take us back to the hotel, I had a binder full of notes from the nutritional sessions, another binder complete with plays and tactics and my head was swimming with the names of the trainers and coaches. I spent most of the night in my room going through the play manuals, trying to get used to where I needed to be in the various situations.

The next morning, we went back into the facility and this time they shuffled the groups. I couldn't detect any method to the madness but they obviously had their reasons and then we skated in a lot of full line drills. Towards the end, we did some extensive one-on-one drills too. Once I figured out what was required, I settled in nicely. Some of the drills were hard for me to do merely because I was so good. I was able to close the gap to the defenseman who was supposed to play the puck before the forechecker got to him. When it was my line's turn, I was able to get to the puck at the same time as the defenseman so it disrupted the flow of the drill. In the end, the coach changed my position so that I didn't get in the way. I'd be the guy on the boards waiting for the pass rather than the guy chasing the puck on the forecheck. During the rest of the drills, I noticed that the coaches paid more attention to who played what role in the drills and usually put me opposite one of the guys who had played in the NHL the previous season.

Similar things happened the next day but the nature of the drills got more physical. One of them was a one-on-one battle of the puck along the boards. The suit really helped me out there, absorbing the majority of the physicality and allowing me to keep going long after even the NHL players were starting to flag. Again, they put me against the good players and I began to see them start to take me seriously as my suit's strength became apparent. And again, I noticed the coaches watching and notes being made on clipboards. They weren't the only ones intrigued. One of the reporters managed to corner me before I could escape.

"Peter! You're having a fantastic training camp. What do you think your chances are of making the team?"

I had no idea how to answer that. "...Good?"

"Oh, c'mon, you're out-working some of those veterans. You must have high expectations?"

Great question. If I say yes, then the story will be that I think I'm better than the vets. "I'm just taking it one day at a time, and doing my best."

"The team has listed you at 300lbs and some of the press think that's a typo and are listing you at 200lbs. Which one is right?"

It had been a long time since I had been 200lbs and just looking at me should have answered that question for him. I answered with a stony face. "Do you have any hockey-related questions?"

"Sure, here's a hockey question for you. There doesn't seem to be much in the way of playing history in the press pack. Where were you playing hockey last year?"

I don't know why but I put on a big smile. When you have something to hide, act like you don't. "I didn't play professionally last year," I told him.

He didn't know whether to take my answer at face value or not. The smile must have bothered him. "Seriously, where did you play? If you didn't play pro here, was it in Europe? Russia?"

I looked over at the press manager who had been hovering nearby. "I don't know what to tell him. I've answered his question

125

but he doesn't believe me. I'm getting on the bus." And then I did just that. When I got back to the hotel, I looked up the news on the training camp and my name was starting to feature prominently, mainly among my fellow training camp attendees in response to the questions "Who is having the best camp?" and "Who's the player to watch?" That felt good. If my peers were recognizing my ability, hopefully the coach and GM were too.

Preseason Game

Then came the day of the first game. They announced in the morning that they obviously couldn't take all sixty players and so they would have to cut some of the players from the camp. I looked around as they read out the names and most of the guys they called were all the young guys - guys who were playing for university teams, rookies who were still playing in the ECHL or similar. And so with fewer players, they could move from four groups to two. These were the expected cuts and so there weren't any looks of surprise or indignation, just acceptance. They headed out the door, presumably to return to the hotel to retrieve their belongings and return to whichever town they would be playing in that season. I had a bolt of realization that if the coach had read out my name, then that would be the end of my little adventure. It would have stopped there and then no amount of negotiation or pleading would have saved me or prolonged my training camp. It was a sobering thought.

We had started with close to sixty players and lost eleven that day. I wondered why they had let them come into the facility on the bus just to turn around and head back to the hotel to pick up their stuff. It seemed a little cruel. I guessed that it didn't matter for those guys who maybe didn't realistically have a chance of sticking with the first team, but still. The bus was full on the way to the game - our opponents were near enough that we could drive there and back in the same day.

I got the nod to be among the 20 players on the roster for the game, so I was excited to be getting my first taste of action. When I looked through the opposition team list though, I frowned. There weren't many NHL players on it. One of the regulars on our team who would be watching from the stands noticed my perplexed look.

"They have to play a certain number of NHL players but just like us, they want to see how well their prospects are developing. And there's always the odd player on a PTO that they want to see in a game, too."

I guessed that as the preseason went on, and the cuts happened more often and the camp size reduced, that this would also be happening with all the other teams in the league. The only real

NHL-level test would be towards the end of the preseason. If I made it that far.

Coach started me on the fourth line. I was centering a line with two young guys who were slated to start in the AHL for the year. They were in only their second professional year and they hadn't been pushing any of the regulars for their spot, so this might be the only shot they got to play against NHL caliber competition this year. The nature of playing the fourth line was that there was a lot of waiting around. You got maybe five to eight minutes in the whole game split across the three periods in 30 to 45 second shifts. So the bad news was that there wasn't much time to make an impact. The good news was that we would be fresh and ready to go each time the coach tapped us.

The first shift was spent chasing the puck on the forecheck. My role was to hang high while the wingers pursued the puck carriers. They did a good job, haranguing and harassing whoever had the puck. Thirty seconds went fast and then we were off. And my first time on an NHL sheet of ice was spent circling high, waiting for a spilled puck or bad outlet pass. So no heroic outcome, no dazzling display of my abilities. Just sticking to the game plan and being ready to pounce on an error. Boring. Safe. Seared into my brain all the same.

C. G. Lambert

The quality of the opposition wasn't incredibly high but to be fair, the team we were fielding wasn't our best either. That manifested itself with lots of coughed up pucks, a lot of misplaced passes and generally broken plays and no flow at all. I was keen to get on the ice but it wasn't until the end of the first period that I found myself changing on the fly after a dump in. I jumped over the boards when our other center came off and I made a beeline for their defenseman who had collected the puck from the corner. The defenseman was isolated because their forwards had also gone for a change, and he saw me barreling towards him at top speed and made the smart choice and passed it to his defense partner and then braced himself for the check. The normal move would have been to finish my check and plaster the poor guy against the boards. But he hadn't put much mustard on the pass and I knew that I could get to the puck before the other defenseman could, so I pivoted instead and lost only a little bit of speed while changing direction. I could see the eyes of the other defenseman widen as he realized that I was going to get the puck first. He started moving toward me but I collected the puck and gave him a head fake, which sent him the wrong way. By then, my two wingers had joined me and found space, both calling for the puck. I sent the puck sizzling to the stick of the winger who had snuck behind the goalie and he tapped it into the undefended goal. Nice.

I got my first goal in the second period but it wasn't against an NHL goalie, so it was hard to feel elated. They had the puck in our zone, we managed to bump it free, I got it and skated the length of the ice and beat the goalie, blocker side low. A breakaway from our own zone? None of their players had come close to me at all. In fact, the whole game had the feel of a scrimmage. I did everything I could to take it seriously but when your line scores four goals in about the same number of minutes of ice time, it tells you something. It certainly told the coach something because we hardly saw the ice at all in the third period.

The press were keen on chatting afterwards. "Were you disappointed in your ice time today? It looked like you were just getting going and the ice time dried up in the third there."

"Coach wanted to see different players and see how they performed and so he gave out the ice time accordingly. Look, I always want to be out on the ice. I love playing, and I think I have a lot to give."

"Four points on such a low ice time though, you must be happy with that?"

"I'll take all the ice time I can get, though preseason points don't matter, so..." I shrugged.

When we got back to the hotel, I looked up the coverage of the game and the coach had gone out of his way to downplay my impact on the game. Which was fair enough, the opposition were very much not NHL caliber but c'mon Coach, a little pat on the back in the press wouldn't hurt, would it?

Some players you mesh with and some you don't. Coaches usually try different line combinations specifically to see if they can find that chemistry. In the beer leagues, for some reason, the players I clicked with more than others were the short guys. I don't know why, maybe a little bit of the mother hen coming out of me, I guess.

Stan Gossberg was one of our rookies who was 5' 9" on a good day. That's 175 cm in metric. Anyway, in the preseason games, he would frequently be one of my wingers on the fourth line. One day after the preseason game, we were in the changing room getting changed. The vibe in the room was confusing - instead of the release of tension after a game or practice, categorized by banter and joking and goofing around, there was a quiet tension in the air. Very understandable I guessed. Careers were being made or broken in real time, so there wasn't a lot of relaxing going on.

While I felt some of the pressure to perform and secure my spot on the opening night roster, my personality was to try and do my bit to make any team I was in a bit more welcoming and fun to be on, especially for the young guys. Even if it was in a professional environment where I was still very much feeling my way around. I noticed Stan looking at the scars on my foot. He looked away quickly, not wanting to be rude.

"Motorcycle crash," I told him. "I came off on the road and only had normal shoes on that came up to below the ankle bone. When I hit the road and skidded along, I got this graze just above the shoe line." He was watching quietly. I pointed to the scars on my knee. "And this one was from a spiral fracture of the tibia and fibula. I tried turning my whole body around the leg which was holding my body weight." He grimaced in sympathy. I then noticed that he had what looked like burns on the inside of his arms. He saw me glance at them and stretched out his arms so that I could see.

"I was in a car crash in Juniors," Stan said.

Instantly I was transported back in time a decade and a half ago. A knock on the door in the middle of the night. A policeman and policewoman with terrible news. A car crash.

Stan continued softly. "It took them an hour to get the jaws of life to me. All the time, the flames were getting closer. The firemen kept spraying them down but they kept creeping closer."

We must have looked a sight, each of us reliving our respective worst memories, his quiet terror matching my silent grief.

"To this day, I can't stand enclosed spaces. I freak out."

I smiled sadly. "I don't blame you at all. So, no camping trips, no sleeping bags?"

He laughed. "More like no tunnels, no crowded elevators. No portaloos."

I looked around at the training facility. "I think you'll be ok with the portaloos. I don't imagine the team will ever give us a portapotty."

"I hope you're right."

We had one day off between games so it was back to the practice facility. On the way down to the bus, I stopped off at the reception desk of the hotel to pick up a newspaper. I wanted to see if there were any stories in the paper that I could clip out for some sort of career scrapbook. When I got to the desk, the receptionist looked up at me. "Ah, you are with the team, yes?"

"Yes, I am."

"Okay, so I have two leaving today, Williams and... Ker... Kerzha—"

"Kerzhakov? Thanks for that." I took a copy of the paper and headed towards the bus. Why did she tell me that? Oh! She must have thought that I was in team management, not a player. And if those two were being cut, then that would explain why she mentioned them. But why would she need to tell a member of team management who was getting cut? Surely everyone who needed to know would have been told by the team? Strange. There was no guarantee that they were getting cut, so there was nothing to be gained by talking to them about it.

When we got to the facility, we had a debrief on the previous day's game and then announced the team for the next preseason game. It was basically all the players who hadn't played that first game, so I would be watching the game from the press box. They then got to those who would be going back to their teams - Simon Williams and Dimitri Kerzhakov. Still no looks of shock or outrage, so I figured that this news wasn't unexpected. It looked like the receptionist was a reliable source for who was being cut. I couldn't imagine a scenario where knowing that would be beneficial in any way but it was always good having something up your sleeve.

Another on-ice session ensued with great speed and stick handling but I was still struggling with where I was supposed to be on the ice. The other part I was slowly improving on was decision-making at such high speeds. I would be skating hard up the ice with the puck and one of the young guys would be trailing slightly behind, sprinting flat out. With a two-on-none, the clever thing to do was to go wide on the goalie which would give you two options - pass to the other player or else take the shot yourself. But with my speed, I found myself a long way in front of my teammate, so I would elect to take the shot. I usually scored in the one-on-one with the goalie but I figured if I slowed down a little, it would allow my teammate to catch up and then I would have the option of passing or shooting, and that should result in a higher scoring chance. When the games started to mean something, that might be the better option.

The next morning, I went back to the reception desk as much to see if I would be told who was getting cut as to pick up a newspaper, if I'm being honest. The receptionist looked up as I arrived and told me that Jiri Nosek would be needing to give back his room key. I smiled and nodded, and thanked her for the information before heading for the bus. Jiri was a Czech guy who had been playing over in Europe, and he'd played in the first game.

I saw him on the bus chatting with one of the rookies as I got on and he was talking about the venue for the game that day, and how he hoped to see the city a little. I made the mistake of reacting to that comment and he saw it.

"What? You don't think that I will get to see the city?"

If I was a smart man, I would have said something like we'd be watching the game from the press box and then heading back home. So we wouldn't be able to see the city because of that. But I am not a smart man and eventually he managed to extract from me the fact that he was going to be sent back to Europe rather than coming with us to watch the game. He didn't look devastated but he still looked disappointed.

When we arrived at the facility for the pre-game meeting prior to getting back on the bus for the trip to our home arena, they announced that Jiri would not be joining us. He got up quickly and accompanied one of the coaching staff to the door. They must have been talking because on the way to the bus, one of the back-office guys pulled me aside for a word.

"Jiri told me that you mentioned that he might be cut. I'm just wondering how you knew that?"

I didn't want to cut off my intelligence from the front desk, so I had to find a reasonably believable way that I might have figured out when he would be cut.

"Per diem!" I said.

"Excuse me?"

"I figured it out from the per diem. You give everyone an envelope of cash when we checked in at the hotel. Jiri mentioned how much his was, which was different from mine and so I figured that you were paying him per day and then I figured out how many days of camp you expected him to stick around."

"Got you. It might be best for everyone if you kept that sort of information to yourself."

"Sure, I only mentioned it to him because he asked and because my per diem runs out soon as well."

"So, does that mean you're going to be cut when the money runs out or does it mean that we give you another per diem?"

I played dumb. "Ah, I hadn't thought of that."

He nodded and then went on his way, so I think I got away with that one.

The Cut

Our home arena was pretty impressive. Obviously you had the retired jerseys in the rafters along with the pennants for all the winning seasons we'd had. There were more fans than there had been in my game and they were loud!

One of the other players on a PTO happened to be standing next to me during the game and struck up a conversation. We were joining the crowd in response to one of our players receiving a particularly heavy hit against the boards, and he gave a sly smile. "I hope he's okay. Although it wouldn't be the end of the world if he pinged his knee."

I looked over in surprise. It was one thing to think those sorts of things, and quite another to say them. To a teammate in our home arena. He kept going.

"Think about it. If he's out of the line-up, there's one more slot available for someone like me or you."

"I guess so. Hey, I'm going to get a drink, do you want anything?"

The weird part of the exchange was that there was no upshot for the guy saying it. At worst, I knew him for putting his own self-interest above the team (although being a professional athlete, you do have to have one eye on your own career) but what was the best-case scenario? What was he trying to achieve?

After the game, we made our way back to the hotel. In the morning, I went back to the reception to see if anyone else was going to be cut. Apparently nobody was going to be but they gave me another envelope of cash. I counted it quickly and did the math. It looked like I was good for another week, which meant that if the per diems matched my ability to avoid the cuts, then I would be good until the last two games of the preseason.

Practice went well and as expected, nobody got cut. We had a debrief on the game and people were starting to get into the routine - game, debrief, practice. They also announced the roster for the next game and again, it was my turn to play.

Fast forward to the game and even though I was on the fourth line again, we got a little more ice time and again, I was productive. Every time we were on the ice, we were dangerous. We generated five points on about ten minutes of ice time before the third period again saw us hardly used.

The scores in the preseason games varied wildly across the league. There were even some double-digit scores as the different teams whittled their non-NHL players from their roosters at different paces, leading to some one-sided matchups during the games. I was just happy to be playing and producing. Surely no one could argue with my abilities if I was generating so much offense while, I hasten to add, being very responsible in the defensive zone as well?

I was surprised to find myself playing the next game. It was against the same team as we had just played but both teams tweaked their rosters. The opposing team's superstar player was now going to be playing and our own roster sported many more first-string players.

In our pregame briefing, Coach told me that I would be marking their star player and that I would be on the third line. Finally, a promotion! It was going to take a little bit of an adjustment though. In beer league, there wasn't much close coverage.

The game itself flew by in a rush and before I knew it, I was surrounded by the normal scrum of reporters with their wide range of questions.

"Peter, over here. A bit of a drop off in point production tonight. What was the difference between the last game and this one?"

I looked at the reporter as if he was stupid before realizing that wasn't nice. I took a second to gather myself. "Coach wanted to see me closely marking their star player. Unfortunately, I wasn't able to stop their line from scoring but I think I did a pretty good job of isolating him and keeping him off his game. The head-to-head battles were great for me to gauge how my game has progressed. I was really happy getting more game time against some really good players."

But inside I was muttering obscenities. When you're focusing on defense, it's hard to generate offense and when you're concentrating on closing down one particular player, your whole world collapses to the few square feet that surrounds that player and where he will be skating next. Scoring becomes an afterthought. I did my job.

The next couple of days involved more cuts and I left the reception desk alone now that I had an indication of how long I might be hanging around as indicated by the size of my per diem envelope. The cuts were beginning to affect players who maybe weren't on the same page as team management with regards to their performance. There were some dark looks and surprised expressions in the meeting room when the latest rounds were announced. For my part, I figured that if there were twenty players on an NHL regular season roster, then the day that there were nineteen other players in training camp I had done my job and had made the team. Until then, the training camp attendee list was a constant countdown to that day. If there were 34 players at camp including me, then that meant that 14 other players needed to be cut for me to make the final roster. That day, I would write 14 on the calendar next to the phone in my hotel room. If six more were cut the next day, then I would write 8 beside that day on the calendar. That number had to hit zero. It just had to.

The coaching staff started to put together specific line combinations and I spent whole practice days with the same players beside me instead of mixing things up drill to drill. We had two days to go until my per diem payments ran out, with two games to complete the preseason on the two days after that, so I was really working hard on my game. Which for me usually meant cramming and trying to learn the tactics from the binders, and talking to the coaching staff about my positioning and the video guys on where I had erred in the games. The number on the calendar had flicked over to four and all the other guys on PTOs had been cut. Things were getting close to the end, one way or the other.

The ever-present press corps were always there to mess with your head.

"You took a few drills on the first line and a few on the second line, where do you think the coach will be playing you? On the first line?"

"I've got to make the roster for those last two games yet so it's a bit premature to talk about what line I'll be on. Are you going to tell Kevin that I'm centering the first line? Those three have great chemistry built up over years and I think if you're the coach, you would have to think twice before breaking that up for any reason. I don't know what the coaching staff have in mind but I think they're seeing where I can fit in."

"Coach has said that nobody's spot on the roster is given and that everybody has a chance. What's it like coming in from the outside?"

"That's all I've known. I'm just focused on me and my performance at the moment because that's all I can control."

"You're on a PTO. Have any other teams reached out if you get cut?"

I blinked. "Actually I've been so laser focused on making the team, I have no idea what I would do if I don't make the cut." I laughed. "So thanks for putting that thought in my head!"

I admit that particular thought now lurked in the darker recesses of my mind for the next couple of days. With the uncertainty of getting through the daily cuts, would I ever settle for playing for a different NHL team than my favorite one? Would any of the other teams offer me a contract based on what I had been able to produce on the ice in the preseason? Would it be enough of a hockey resume that Sonny had mentioned in that pub all those days ago?

After due consideration, I decided that I would come to that decision when I needed to and I would, of course, concentrate on making the opening roster of my first-choice team. I needed to focus on that. But I also knew that should my efforts be in vain, that my agent would probably not find it too difficult to find me a home on a rebuilding team. Maybe even for more money. That should have given me some comfort but it really didn't. This was the team I wanted to play for.

It was with great relief that I got my per diem envelope for the last two days of the preseason. I chose to believe that that meant that I was in the team but one of the training staff put me right on that.

"Oh, no. We just pay the per diem to the end of the preseason for everybody at this point. We've still got three players to cut before game one, so it's just easier operationally to make sure that everyone is covered until then. I'm sorry if you read anything into that."

The second to last game of the preseason and I was back in shut down mode, centering the third line and tasked with shutting down the opposition's star player. This time, my wingers were more skilled so I had greater success keeping our opponent's line off the scoreboard. This time, there were no impertinent questions, mainly because one of our players had a particularly good game, so they were flavor of the day. It was interesting, I thought, as I watched the media scrum surround the player who had scored a hattrick, how the scoreboard only told one story of the game, and how that story represented a true face of the game that had been played. But there were many different faces to other equally true stories of the game. Like my case of the player told to closely mark a particular opponent where success is represented by a zero in every stat for the game. And then there was the fourth line, who likewise kept the opponents off the scoreboard whenever they were on the ice, who forechecked hard and energetically and secured the puck for offensive zone faceoffs for our first and second lines to come on and convert that pressure into goals, whose own success would maybe show up in the takeaways exceeding the giveaways for the game. Don't get me started on the defensemen. Sure, there's a stat called plus/minus which is calculated by counting the number of times that you're on the ice when your team scores and then removing the number of times that you're on the ice when the opposition scores. That gives some insight into the defensive roles of forwards, and shows the success of defensemen in keeping the puck out of our own net. You only count the goals that aren't scored on the powerplay, so it does go some way to paint the picture of the hidden game that easier stats like goals and assists don't show.

But I knew that the press saw my plus/minus of zero and passed it over for the more sexy stats of Kevin's three goals scored, as well as the marginally less sexy stats of shots (10) and shooting accuracy (30%). It sounds like I was bent out of shape by Kevin's success. That I was the only one who could be successful. That's not true. I just wanted to point out that the coach's assignment meant that only some players were eligible for the limelight.

So how would I get the coach to give me the assignments which could lead to the success that I knew I was capable of? From what I had pieced together from conversations with the veterans and the coaching staff, you had to prove that you could play defensive, responsible hockey. That meant getting back to playing defense when the opposition had the puck. It was tempting for lazy forwards to hang high and hope that one of their teammates could get them the puck. The only problem with that was that the magic pass they were expecting had to somehow get through the entire opposition. Which could lead to a one on zero with the goalie but it would more likely lead to a scoring opportunity the other way. After all, the lazy player would be taking themselves out of the defensive effort, leading to a four on five situation.

So, I had to impress the coach with my two-way play. And then amaze the Coach with my offensive potential. Which not only meant scoring goals, but also setting up goals for my teammates. If you got a reputation for being a selfish player who always chose to shoot the puck instead of passing to a teammate, then the goalie would know that you would be shooting and could concentrate on blocking your shot rather than having to double think about whether you were going to shoot or pass to someone else. At the other end of the scale, it was easy to dither too much and make one too many passes. Where you placed yourself on the shoot/pass scale was something that coaches certainly noticed.

And so on to the last game of the preseason. I was dropped down to the fourth line for the game. I couldn't tell whether this was driven by a negative opinion about my last game or if it was due to the structure of our opposition not having such a standout star player as the opposition had in the previous game. The freedom of not being locked into countering a star player was invigorating and I was flying around on the forecheck, hitting everything that moved and enjoying every one of the few minutes that I was on the ice. We generated a lot of turnovers and were able to convert a couple of them, leading to me ending the game with two goals on broken plays.

Coming off the ice, I wasn't surprised that the press wanted to speak to me but I was surprised by what they were interested in talking about.

"You've won the Best Rookie in Training Camp award for the year, how do you feel?"

I cocked an eyebrow at him. "You know that I don't count as a rookie, right? I'm too old."

"That's the league rules for the Calder. The team votes for this award, not the league, and they're giving it to you."

"Does this mean that I've definitely made the starting roster?"

The bonhomie and laughing in the press room died down a little at that question. "Uh... no, sometimes the player winning that award starts in the AHL."

C. G. Lambert

I dialed my smile down by 50%. "Well, in that case, I'd like to thank my teammates for the award, for making me feel welcome and for helping me adjust to the pace of the game. I hope I can stick around and contribute in the regular season."

Game One

"I'm standing with Peter Collins, the 40-year-old rookie who has had quite the first professional game. A goal twenty seconds into the second period. Is that the fastest goal you've scored?"

"I remember scoring one in eight seconds."

"Oh? Okay. Talk us through the goal."

"I was playing wing; our center lost the draw and the puck squirted out and stopped halfway to their defenseman. I got away from my winger and was going to get to the puck first. The defenseman lined me up and I knew he would hit me a second after I got the puck. Our other winger was cutting up the center of the ice, calling for a pass, but I could see that their other defenseman was all over him. A pass would be a low chance play, so I elected to dump the puck on net to see if our winger could get to the rebound before their defenseman. So I flicked the puck into the air, just before the defenseman hit me. I go down and start to get up but the ref is already indicating a goal. My dump-in was supposed to hit the goalie in the pads and bounce out in front for our other winger to collect but it accidentally landed on its edge and bounced over the goalie's stick and between his pads, slotting perfectly through the tiny gap. I took the hit to make the play." I looked over to the reporter to see a frozen smile.

"Thanks for that. No, I meant could you talk us through the goal in the second period."

"Oh, right, sorry. Yeah, I lost the draw but our winger managed to get in on the forecheck and put a lot of pressure on their defenseman. I came up the middle of the ice and got into the passing lane, and was lucky enough to intercept the D-to-D pass."

"Why didn't you shoot on net straight away?"

"I knew that our other winger would be crashing the net and I thought the backdoor tap-in would have a higher chance as I thought the goalie was slightly over-playing the shot. I was right about that but when he pushed off to cover the pass, he wasn't strong enough on his stick and accidentally turned the puck into the net."

"So a bit of a flukey goal there but it must be nice to get on the board."

"Absolutely, it's taking a little bit longer to get used to the pace and size of the ice but the coaching staff are working with me and we're making great progress."

"Any comment about starting on the fourth line?"

"Everyone has to earn their ice time. I have to prove that I'm going to be a safe pair of hands and play responsible 200 feet hockey. I love getting in on the forecheck, it really plays to my strengths."

"Gary in the booth is just feeding me some stats. Your fourth line was really able to push the tempo and you kept them cooped up in their own zone for significant portions of the game."

"Yeah, my wingers are great energy guys and we play high tempo hockey which is a lot of fun."

"Were you surprised when the coach gave you some shifts with the third line?"

"You never want to see anyone get hurt or injured but Coach told me I was the next man up and it was great getting the additional ice time."

"And productive too, you managed to get a couple of assists. Not a bad start to the season."

"Happy for the win."

"Thanks, Peter."

"Thanks."

Then I headed into the locker room. I was fortunate that none of the guys had heard my interview and the slight faux pas about talking about the wrong goal. I was sure that they would give me a hard time when they heard about it.

Every team has a token - a hat or something to celebrate the man of the match. As the guys took off their gear, there was the usual joking and a relaxed vibe as everyone enjoyed the win. Being game one, there had been a lot of focus to start the season well but there wasn't any of the pressure that comes when you are on a losing streak. So it was very relaxed.

The coach got everybody's attention.

"Great start guys. Really impressive and well done to our rookies. Especially Peter. Three points in your first game."

I didn't want to attract any undue attention so accepted the token and shook his hand. The rest of the team were looking expectantly at me so I assumed that it was necessary to give a speech. I didn't want the limelight too soon in the season even if I had played well, so keep it brief.

"Thanks guys. Great way to start the season. Cheers."

There was a smattering of polite applause and then we went back to the normal decompression which happened after the game.

The Forty Year Old Rookie

I grabbed a shower and got changed, making sure the equipment guys got my suit into my gear bag as soon as it came off. And just like that, my first professional game was over.

The other players were all dressed very smartly in suits, and I had noticed that earlier on in the preseason. My efforts were less impressive, a combination of having a different body shape and the fact that they were sporting tailored suits made to measure, while my selection was a single department store suit. So while the rest of my teammates could have stepped out of the pages of GQ or Men's Vogue, I was a little more aligned with the fans, sartorially.

The wave of fans leaving the stadium had died down to a trickle of the die-hards and those who had stopped off for a beer after the game, and so as I made my way to the underground, the streets were almost back to normal. I could have taken a train and then a bus but it would have taken me two hours to get home. Instead, I went as far as the underground ran and then got an Uber the rest of the way. It still took an hour but it gave me a chance to decompress.

If I thought things had been moving quickly during the preseason, the time between the last game of the preseason and the beginning of the regular season had gone by in the blink of an eye. The day after the last preseason game, I had marched down to the reception desk of the hotel and almost demanded to know which players would have to give their passcards back. By my calculations, there were still three cuts to be made and only two days to make them before our first regular season game. I almost sobbed with relief when I was told three names, none of which were mine. So much relief. I had to concentrate so I wasn't grinning like a Cheshire Cat during breakfast. That day, we all went into the training facility and they gave the players that were being cut the bad news. This speech was more genuine than the others had been, with a more of a heartfelt plea to keep up the good work and that they would find themselves with opportunities during the season. The reasons for those opportunities were not spelled out, because that would involve poor play or injury for one of the other players in the room.

Again, I had to really pinch myself to prevent grinning like a gormless idiot and giggling to myself that I had made the first team, that I was a professional ice hockey player and that I was going to play in the show. I remember nothing about the practice. I must have attended it and done the drills but when I think back to that day, all I recall is the players who were cut leaving the meeting room and then I was opening the door to the hotel room afterwards.

Then I got the call from my agent. "You sitting down, Peter? Congratulations, their GM has made the offer that I told you he would. There's not a lot of wriggle room here, so if you're happy to play for them, we'll get you to sign the documents electronically now and then get some copies printed out for you to sign in the GM's office tomorrow for the cameras. You've done it, Peter! Well done! How do you feel?"

"Wooooh! Yes! Excellent. Thanks for that! I really appreciate your help in this. Awesome. Yes, I feel good. Send through the contract and I'll sign it."

When it came through, I checked that the terms of the contract matched with my recollection of the meeting with the agent. Yup, it was all there: $775k in the majors, $80k in the minors with $1.5M in potential bonuses; so I signed it. Then I ran up and down the halls like a lunatic. I thought of who I could tell and came up blank. Sure, I could have texted some of my teammates but it wouldn't really be appropriate for me to go out drinking to celebrate this close to the start of the regular season, would it? I could just see the reports should anything untoward occur.

Instead, I steadied my breathing and tried to distract myself. I had a bit of cash left and I would be able to stay in the hotel at the team's expense for a bit longer. When they said I was on my own, I guess I could stay at the same hotel and just pay cash until that ran out. Hopefully my first pay would come through before my cash ran out. But then after that, I should be set?

When the team announced the signing, my phone blew up with all of my teammates sending me congratulatory texts. When they saw me while we waited for the bus, there were lots of handshakes and slapping of shoulders, a really nice welcoming vibe. It felt good and totally at odds with the awkwardness when I had first arrived at camp and been challenged by the guy with the clipboard before I could even get on the bus!

The next day, there was a press conference and photos taken of the GM and myself signing the contract. I'd already digitally signed the real contract but this was the ceremonial signing. It reminded me of the husband and wife signing documents after the wedding, and that analogy stretched as far as the questions from the press.

"GM, you've found a star player that no one else managed to find. How did the signing come about?"

How did you two meet?

"Well, we have an extensive network of scouts both here and in Europe, in both amateur and professional leagues, but we also have very strong relationships with agents. Peter's agent reached out and made a pretty impassioned pitch for why we should invite Peter along for a PTO, and I am very glad we did."

The best man introduced us.

"You were very close to the ceiling of the cap. How did you manage to fit a player of Peter's caliber under the cap?"

How did you seal the deal?

"We typically have a small amount of cap space that grows by the end of the season for additional help at the trade deadline. We decided to move pretty quickly when it became apparent what Peter was capable of. We'll have the rest of the season to decide whether we need to make that space available in other ways but with regards to Peter's deal, there was really only one deal that could be made and we were both keen on making it."

I made her an offer she couldn't refuse.

"But why this team, Peter? Surely you could have gotten more money from any of the rebuilding teams?"

What was it about her that made you pop the question?

"Yes, that's true. But I grew up supporting this team. Whenever I was in town, I would try and get tickets to see a game and each season, I followed their progress. I was and always will be a fan. So when the opportunity to play in the league came about, there was really only one choice. I'm glad that we could iron out a deal and that I'll be playing here for the season."

I tried to keep on an even keel, to remind myself this wasn't even halfway through my adventure - that the season was long and arduous, that there would be many more challenges on their way, and that I was in constant danger of being found out. But whenever I was alone, I would break into the biggest smile and have to restrain myself from punching the air and yodeling. The worst was when I was in lifts with mirrored doors. I'd realize I was alone and break into some sort of dance and then catch sight of myself. I would want to stop myself but I also wanted to enjoy the unbridled joy. It had been a long time since I had felt anything like it. Who knew how long it would last?

Performance

The team had a long-standing relationship with the emergency services of the city. This manifested itself in team trips to one of the chapter houses of the fire department. We hung out, helped them make the evening meal and shot the breeze with the crews. The players were leaving the chapter house when one of the vets corralled me and the other rookies and took us for a beer. As we settled into the booth, he turned to me and asked what I thought about the visit.

I looked around the table and grinned. "Pretty cool, got to love that pole, right?"

One of the other guys laughed. "It was a pity they didn't have a call out while we were there. We could have jumped on the back of the truck and checked out a fire."

The vet chuckled and took a sip of his beer. "Yeah, they're a good crew. I've been going there for the last five years." He looked at me.

"Any ideas why the team has that relationship with the fire department?"

I thought about the question for a while. "Well... they're iconic in the city, right? A great way to reinforce that the team belongs here."

The vet shrugged. "Maybe."

One of the rookies wiped his mouth. The beer mustache would be the only one he would have for a little while. "It's a good photo op, right?"

"Not quite. Well, a bit I guess, those helmets of theirs are huge! No, it's to teach all of us a lesson in humility."

"What do you mean?"

"What do we do for a living?"

"We play hockey"

"Exactly. We play a game and we get paid a lot of money."

"Some more than others," laughed one of the rookies.

"Sure, but even you rookies are getting paid a hell of a lot more than any of the firefighters. And if you compare us, we both need to be in great shape. We are both paid for what we physically do. But compare us playing our game with them running into a building on fire. Which is more important to society? So I know you've spent the last ten years of your lives being the star players and getting all the girls and having the coaches and schools all bend over backwards because you're all that. But in this city, even if we play well, we aren't heroes. Those guys back there are the heroes. Always remember that." There was a contemplative silence in the booth as we considered his words.

We only had one beer - this was in the regular season after all, so not long after that, people all headed for the door. The vet and one of the rookies left together and I must have had a quizzical look on my face as I clocked that. One of the other rookies, Jason, noticed this and paused to explain.

"The rookie is living with the vet."

"Oh! Okay, that makes sense."

"Yeah, he gets the stability of a solid family life and management knows he's not off banging models and getting high. Plus, it's cheaper than a hotel or living in an apartment when you're only there half the time."

"True. I think Sidney Crosby lived with Mario Lemieux when he came into the league. Where are you staying?"

The rookie looked rueful. "Management hasn't given me the word to start looking yet, so I'm in a Holiday Inn."

"What do you mean?"

Jason frowned at my ignorance. "I'm a rookie, right? You know at the start of the season when you can still play ten games and not have it count towards your contract? Well, since there's so much shuffling up and down, everyone is in a state of chaos. When the back office decides that you'll be sticking to the top team for the rest of the season, barring injuries or a run of bad play, of course, they give you a ring and say 'find a permanent place for the rest of the season.' That's the call you want to get."

"And what about the next season?"

The rookie took his time answering. "I don't remember much from high school." I hid my surprise. This kid was out of school for, what, one? Two years? "But I remember one lesson in science class. Inertia. There was some law - a bunch of laws - but basically it boiled down to if something is there, unless some force operates on it, it's going to stay there. So once you make it to the big league and they give you the call, then there's a good chance you'll be there the next season, and the next season."

"So you're looking forward to that call from the coach?"

"It will be the GM or one of his assistants. And no, you can't look forward to that call, because it might be 'hey, you can look for an apartment' or it might be 'hey, we've traded you to a loser team for a six pack and a bucket of pucks.' Or even 'hey, we're sending you down to the farm team, report to the bus stop.'"

"So how come that rookie gets to stay with the vet?"

"Oh, he was always going to stick this season."

"Why's that?"

"First round draft pick."

"Huh? So he's good enough to get picked in the first round. So what?"

Jason gave me an appraising look before answering. "I keep forgetting this is your first year in the pros. That guy was picked in the first round three years ago. He's been playing in the minors since then, getting better and better, putting up some good numbers. There were a few concerns around his game and by getting a whole bunch of ice time, he has proven that he can play. But the press hate the fact that they have been so slow bringing him up to the bigs and the pressure has been building. So they want to make sure he has every chance of staying. They're giving him the royal treatment. A vet to stay with. He's got a built-in lift to practice and games. He doesn't have to cook."

"What round did you go in?"

"Me? Seventh. The last round. I've earned everything the hard way. But it means they can do what they like with me. No pressure for me to be a star, right? If I get five minutes a night and score five goals a season, they can say 'well, what do you expect, he's a seventh rounder.' But that guy there? I've got a hundred bucks that says he averages fourteen minutes a game this season, and there's no way he's on the checking line. They'll put him with guys who are going to score." All this was said with a smile.

"You're not bitter?"

"It's the game. It's how it is. It's not going to change if I have a little cry now, is it?"

"You must hate me then. I come in and take one of the slots that should go to one of you young guys."

"It's hard to hate someone with your wheels and your shot. You have zero idea of where you're supposed to be which is hilarious. But you always get back in time to lift the stick or block the shot or intercept the pass. That and when you check someone they stay checked!"

I laughed along with him. At least one person was on my side.

Early in the regular season, Stan got his chance with the first team when we had a couple of injuries. Naturally enough, they started him on the fourth line as an energy line. I went out of my way to look after him on the ice and that led to one memorable incident when there was a pile up in the corner with bodies all over the place and I went wading in, pulling guys off until I could see Stan and pulling him to his feet.

"You ok?"

He blinked and nodded, and we skated away. The fact that I was pulling guys out of the pile concerned the refs for a second and they hovered nearby, expecting me to start swinging at the opposing team's players, but once they realized I was just digging Stan out of the pile, they relaxed.

I spent the entire training camp and preseason adjusting to the pace of the NHL. Even during the first weeks of the regular season, I was still finding my feet. That manifested itself in a series of embarrassing and regrettable incidents, the frequency of which diminished as I found my game in the league. I wasn't putting a lot of pressure on myself to perform, and I think that this relaxed attitude certainly helped me in games. It definitely helped me to laugh off the incidents. Even though the suit had a feedback loop to detect my body motion and balance and adjusted according to the programming I had made, it still wasn't perfect.

One game early in the season, I was making my way back to the bench after my shift during a stoppage in play and I happened to look up in the stands. When I twisted to look at the upper stands on the other side of the ice, the suit misinterpreted my motion and I ended up taking a tumble onto the ice. Having twenty thousand people laughing at you sounds like an atrocious experience but for me, it was no big deal. Just a sign that I was no longer falling over on the ice in front of twenty people. By the time I made it to the bench, I had a big grin on my face and laughed along with the rest of the team as they gave me a ribbing. It was easy to laugh it off when my being a klutz didn't have any impact on the result of the game.

Anyone can catch an edge or blow a tire - that's when you end up lying on the ice because of a misstep in your skating. It could be that one of your legs clip the other as you stride or that your skate goes into a rut in the ice and turns what your body expects to be a smooth glide into a slight wobble which you don't recover from. Or it could be that your skate blade is very sharp and it accidentally grips the ice unexpectedly, throwing you off balance. Even someone who had been skating since the age of five and was in their tenth year of professional hockey could go down when pushing their skating as far as it would go.

I had just been given the third star of the game in the second week of the season and went out on the ice to acknowledge the crowd. The lights were out in the arena and the spotlight followed me for my little turn. The bright light stopped me from seeing the cable on the ice from the ice level cameraman filming me and so he got a great closeup of me taking a tumble as I skated over the cable and landed on my face right in front of him. The look of surprise made it onto a large number of 'plays of the week' videos on the internet for that week and then the plays of the month videos after that.

The press always brought those up in the post-game interviews. "You took a little tumble out there."

"Yes, the opposing team were having trouble stopping me, so it looks like they got their broadcast team in on the act," I replied with a smile after the third star spill. "Look, when you're playing at the pace that I am, you're not always going to be in control," I said after blowing a tire coming around the net on a break out. "The good news is by the time I got back on my feet, I was already in position to defend after we turned the puck over in the neutral zone."

The team all piled on, giving me a hard time and as the season went on, I think it made the other players more relaxed. If I wasn't perfect, it meant that they didn't have to be either and if I was pushing myself beyond my abilities, then that encouraged them to push themselves hard as well.

The Apartment

After I had made the team and played for a couple of weeks, one of the back-office guys came up to me after a game and introduced himself.

"Bryan Smith, Travel and Accommodations Manager. It looks like you'll be up in the big team for the rest of the season and I've been tasked with finding you a place to live. Let me know whether you want to buy or rent, what your budget is and where you want to live, and I'll find you a list of candidate properties and we can take it from there."

I was a bit taken back. I didn't realize the call that I had been hoping for would actually happen in person. I knew the hotel I was staying in must have been expensive but I was expecting to be kicked out and left to fend for myself rather than having Bryan around to help me with the leg work.

"Do you want to grab a coffee? I have so many questions!"

"Sure, let's go."

When we were suitably caffeinated, the interrogation began.

"Rent or buy?"

I thought about what might happen if the salary stopped for whatever reason, and there were a lot of reasons why it might stop. Being found out with the suit, injury... okay, there were maybe only two reasons but having a million-dollar mortgage when the money dried up didn't seem like a sound financial decision.

"Uh.. rent, definitely rent. No long-term leases, either."

He looked up sharply at that. I shrugged.

"Players get traded."

He accepted that and made a note on his clipboard.

"Near the arena, near the practice facility or somewhere else?"

I frowned. "Where else would people stay?"

Bryan smiled. "You'd be surprised. We had one player who wanted to stay in the center of town, a little way from the arena but right in the bright lights of downtown. He wanted his finger on the pulse. But even he found it hard to relax with so much stimulation down there."

"Where do the other players stay?"

"There are some of the older guys who have bigger places that they bought a little way from the practice facility but most of the guys live pretty close."

"Okay, let's do that too."

"How many bedrooms do you need?"

"Just one." I thought about how much I might save if I went with a studio instead of a one bedroom but then I remembered my biweekly salary. "Yeah, one bedroom."

"Do you need any other facilities? A swimming pool? Gym? Carpark?"

"If I'm near here, then I guess I won't need the gym or the pool. Just the carpark."

He gave me a range of rents for those sorts of apartments, from the run of the mill ten-year-old complexes all the way to the brand-new glistening glass and steel types. I gave him the range of rent that I'd be willing to pay and then he thanked me for my time and said he'd have a list to have a look at online by the end of the day.

For a while, the tech giants like your Yahoos and your Googles and Facebooks and what nots would have offices with everything you might need - free food, massages, haircuts, foosball. That was to make sure you spent as much time as possible in the office. Even if you weren't doing work every hour that you were there, they kept you there as much as possible so that they got all of your discretionary effort.

I'm not saying that the team was like that at all. Those tech giants were about squeezing as much out of their employees as they could. My NHL team, on the other hand, wanted you to have every opportunity to train and be the best player you could be. Yet, while the training facility operated all year long, there were rules that said the team couldn't coach players during the offseason. So the team was all about giving you everything you needed to maximize your performance during the season, and to maintain and improve in the offseason.

So there were omelets and smoothies. There were the cold baths and recovery massages. There were on-ice and off-ice gym facilities.

I got a reputation pretty early on for having a great work ethic. I'd come into the training facility early and stay late. I'd put in extra time with the video guy and chat with the trainers. I remember seeing one of the coaches nudging one of the rookies during the season and pointing to me and whispering. I knew that I was being singled out, not only as being a great performer on the ice, but also as someone who put the time in off the ice as well. But the truth of it was that I was lonely and bored. Before my professional ice hockey career, when I was working in an office or from home, I would finish work by 6pm and be mentally exhausted, and have something to eat and then relax. If it was a hockey night, I would go to a game. If it was one of those years where my team actually practiced, then we might have a late-night session to get to. Otherwise, it was a computer game, watching a movie or TV and then bed. I would have social interactions with my teammates or roommates or workmates, even if that was only online. Maybe I'd go out to see a movie or just grab a beer with some friends.

But when I went pro, there were no friends. There were no roommates because the flat had been blown up. So that just left the team. I knew no one outside the team either. I didn't have a regular schedule to meet people by taking lessons or doing a hobby, so my whole life revolved around the practice facility. And since I had the suit, my skill level wasn't something that could be improved, I wasn't required to put in the effort to maintain my skills.

So the only reason I was spending so much time there was because I was bored and lonely. And most importantly, I was treated very, very well. By everyone. You could hear it in their voices and how they spoke to you. That was worth the twenty-minute walk from my apartment to the facility. I could have bought a car. I could have bought a very nice car. But putting that sort of money (plus insurance and upkeep) in for the five-minute drive to and from the facility didn't really make much sense, so I kept putting off utilizing the car park in the basement of the apartment building. In hindsight, maybe I shouldn't have gotten an apartment with a car park. I might have saved some money!

I made sure I rotated my attention through the staff to spread myself around, and by and large, I think it worked well. I got to know everybody really well which was great on the whole personal level. It's always good when you walk into a space and feel comfortable and everyone makes eye contact and smiles and chats. I learned a lot about people and remembered what people told me. That was incredibly self-reinforcing - everybody responds well when other people remember things about them. It helped that I had time on my hands and a relaxed attitude towards everything. A trainer comes up to me a little embarrassed, looking for an autograph for a niece who was a fan. No problem. Let's get her on the phone and I'll have a chat with her for a bit.

The best part was with my teammates. They all learned that I would probably be at the practice facility so if someone wanted to work on their shot or their one-on-ones or any other part of their game, then I would be there to help out. I would never give any advice though, even if they asked directly. I'd refer them to the coaching staff. They would inevitably look at me funny as if I was holding out on some secret or trick that I didn't want to share but I would tell them that what worked for me probably wouldn't work for them, and that the trainers and coaches would have insights into the best way to do whatever it was. That would set them up better for the future. The truth was that I didn't know what they would be looking for. The question, "How do I come out of this turn skating faster than I am now?" shouldn't be answered by something like "Tweak the code which powers the suit."

It also spread the word that I was working hard in my own time on my game and the game of my teammates because they would always say to the staff, "I was working on my shot for tip ins with Peter and I wanted to know what you thought about…" whatever it was.

Anyway, the apartment that I decided on was small and convenient for public transport. It wasn't flashy. It came fully furnished and was comfortable. The decor was somewhere between "divorced dad" and "middle range Airbnb". But the most important part was that it was a walkable distance to the training facility.

I had no idea what the future held for me and so I was definitely interested in saving my salary from the game. I had nothing from my life before turning pro, so I was very much starting from scratch at the ripe old age of forty. My savings and pensions were nothing to write home about, so I was being very strict about saving as much of my pay as possible and that meant forgoing a flash car and bling apartment for walking and the most sedate one-bedroom place possible. I admit it was underwhelming. Few people saw it, obviously, but the one time one of the rookies came by on the way to go out for a drink on one of our days off, he looked around confused. If I was the poster child for what you could achieve if you buckled down and worked hard, the rewards were not shown as being financial.

"You're not tempted to stay someplace nicer?" he asked.

I smiled. "I'm one injury away from the end of a career which has only just begun. I can't really afford too much bling."

"At least let me introduce you to my tailor. You can't keep turning up in off the rack suits."

And that's how I found myself spending a couple of grand on two custom suits. It shows how my frame of reference had not adjusted to my new earning ability. I thought of that purchase in terms of how many months of rent payments they would be, rather than appreciating that it was less than ten percent of one fortnight's pay. I would do things like have separate bank accounts for my rent and savings and spending money, and I would put the whole year's worth of rent money into that account and then not touch it. I had very few outgoings and again, I would carve out the amounts for the internet, power, phone and heat for the year and put that money into accounts that I never touched afterwards. My agent had said that he could put me in touch with an independent financial advisor if I wanted, someone who wouldn't be giving them a kickback or a commission or anything like that, but I just wanted to see my accounts in a healthy state for once.

The Kids

We went out to a local rink to teach one of the kid's teams out there. There were three of us - me, Stefan who was one of the vets and Adam who was in his first year - accompanied by one of the media handlers. The media wrangler had obviously been in contact with the equipment manager because we each had a pair of gloves and our skates, and we put them on in the bleachers overlooking the rink as the kids went through their warm-ups. The visit had been sprung on us at the last minute - the schedule had said there was some sort of community outreach but nothing more specific than that, so of course I didn't have my special suit. So it was with some trepidation that I laced up my skates. I just hoped nobody was expecting a masterclass in NHL-level skating or shooting. Or anything really.

A couple of the kids on the ice had spotted us as they did their laps and there was a little bit of nudging and pointing before their coach got them back into the drills. They weren't the only ones noticing us as I saw a few of the parents looking between their phones and our faces as we got ready.

When we were ready, we got on the ice and joined the coach. He blew his whistle.

"Okay everyone, grab a knee."

The players must have been ten or eleven. All skinny kids, there must have been a full team worth - maybe twenty-five players, a good smattering of races, and maybe five or six girls.

"We've got some real live NHL players here today to help you with a few drills."

The kids all looked at each of us in turn, trying to figure out who we were. The penny dropped for them and the grins grew really large when they got to me. I guess I was pretty recognizable. We broke up into little groups and started a passing drill. I tried to make sure my passes were as accurate as possible and crisp and hard but without the suit, they were as accurate as my beer league days, as in on the tape of the recipient's stick maybe ten percent of the time, close enough fifty per cent of the time and in the same vicinity the remaining forty percent of the time. I tried to cover by yelling things like "Reach for it" and "Skate onto the pass" in my best coach-voice.

The Forty Year Old Rookie

I caught Stefan's eye after one particularly wayward pass and he gave me a wry grin. I returned it and shrugged. Just a bit of fun, right? But if my poor performance was possibly going to be noticed, I decided that I would hide it by doing less and talking more. So in the shooting drills, I made a point of buzzing around the kids as they did the shooting and passing, giving a lot of positive feedback but not really doing any of the drills. I noticed that Adam was doing the opposite, hot-dogging and showing off what he could do, which in a lot of ways drew attention away from me which was good. On the way off the ice after we had finished, I noticed that the audience had expanded somewhat. The parents on the bleachers had been joined by an assortment of younger girls, some wearing figure skates and some not, loitering near the gate to the ice. They ignored me and Stefan when we came off the ice but closed around Adam, holding out pens and paper for him to sign. The media wrangler had to come down and escort him away to allow him to get his skates off.

I was watching as I unlaced my own and was interrupted by a smooth voice to my left.

"Ah, they found a new toy."

"Hmm? Who?"

"The rink rats. The lovely young ladies down there. Each of them can smell a player just starting his career. They all hope that he'll take a liking to them and then they can latch their claws into him and away they go - never having to work again!"

I half turned to see a handsome woman dressed impeccably, watching me closely.

"Occupational hazard, I guess…?"

"Felicity. Felicity Monroe. That's mine down there - number fifteen. Mark."

"Nice to meet you, Felicity. I'm—"

"I know who you are," she said with a grin. "It strikes me that those girls might be better trying their luck with you. Single rookie lighting up the league. What forty-year-old could resist a gaggle of teens?" She raised a perfectly groomed eyebrow.

"Yeah, I don't think so," I said, returning to my laces.

"But you are single?"

"I am indeed."

"Well, that won't be for long. There's never been a professional athlete that has stayed undiscovered by models, actresses or…" she inclined her head towards the scrum at the side of the ice.

"I'm just focusing on my game at the moment, Felicity. Besides, I would also like to keep out of jail. Some of them look very young."

"At the risk of sounding flirtatious, would you be more interested in someone your own age?"

I looked up and she was watching me evenly. She looked like she had stepped out of a department store's fashion pages. If she'd had work done, it was done well. No trout pout, no unnatural skin tightening, maybe fewer lines around the eyes and mouth than you would expect. I paused before answering, unsure if I was being propositioned or if we were just making conversation.

"I'm afraid I'm not much of a catch. I'm playing well, sure, but I'm not making much more than our young friend down there. My career could end at any time."

"Oh, please. A professional athlete at your age? The divorcees will be queueing around the block. Dating at forty is pretty dire. It's all used car salesmen or men who've been caught with the babysitter or secretary. Besides, dating an NHL player is something to boast about when they're at book club over their third merlot." There was a gleam in her eye as she spoke.

"You're very kind," I managed. I really felt like a lamb, gamboling through the pasture and having a nice innocent conversation with a wolf. A very attractive wolf, with a nice string of pearls which matched her perfect smile, but still a wolf. Holding my skates in one hand, I stood up and extended my other hand to clasp hers briefly. "It was very nice to meet you, Felicity. All the best in the dating world." I managed to grab my gloves and turn without falling over my feet and headed down the stairs to catch up with my teammates as we were ushered out the front doors of the rink.

When we were safely in the minivan and heading back towards the highway, I nudged Adam. "They seemed to like you!"

He grinned good naturedly. "Yeah, it was like that in the last few years in juniors too. You kind of let it bounce off you."

Stefan clasped him on the shoulders. "Good for you, rook. The last thing you want is to be caught up in all that." He looked over at me. "But it looks like you weren't the only one getting some attention."

The rookie looked over, delighted. "Slay! I didn't see that. Were you feasting on the yummy mummies?"

I shook my head. "I guess it was the first time I can say that I've had some attention from hockey."

Stefan blinked. "Really?"

With the amount of data about players freely available, I knew that he was 35, married with two kids, 3 and 5, and had been with his wife for at least ten years. "When did the girls stop screaming for you?"

The Forty Year Old Rookie

He smiled as he looked over his shoulder at me. "Every year there's a new batch of rookies, and by the time you're settled into the first team, you usually have a serious girlfriend so you're pretty much not a target by the time you're in your mid-twenties. But there are some persistent ladies who won't take no for an answer until they see a ring on your finger and sometimes not even then. When you're earning so much more than the people they hang around with, a single night of weakness leading to a pregnancy will be a nice little earner for them." He faced the front again and nudged the rookie. "So keep it wrapped, you don't want any distractions when you're playing. A paternity test and having to pay child support for eighteen years when you're not much more than that yourself can really play with your mind. Oh, and that child support amount is based on your income. So if your contract rate goes down, the child support payments don't go down. So that can really sting."

The rookie nodded respectfully. "Got it."

I shared a look with the vet. Was the rookie just giving us lip service? That's the trouble with experience: it's never appreciated by those who haven't earned it.

I had never been a star player before. Even in my best beer league season where I had led my team in scoring (two of the teams in the league had new goalies, so scoring was up that year, plus the two players better than me on our team had work commitments limiting their availability), we just rolled our three lines of forwards so then everyone got the same ice time.

In the pickup game in Kinnesawa, I had proved myself enough to get into the training camp. In training camp, I had proved myself enough to convert the PTO into a contract. In the preseason, I had proved myself enough to make the opening night roster, even if only on the fourth line. In the first four games, I scored a couple of goals and added seven assists. That made everybody sit up and take notice. I played with joyful abandon, throwing my body around and skating my tail off. I slowly worked out where I was supposed to be and got fewer featured sessions with the video coaches. The rest of the team were impressed when I would block shots but there was no honor in it. Blocking shots is dangerous - you're deliberately putting your body in a shooting lane, while your opponent launches a disk of vulcanized rubber at over 100mph. Sure you've got pads but pads can't cover every part of the body. So when a player slides to block the shot, it's a noble act because they're risking injury to reduce the scoring opportunity.

Normally. When I did it, I got the praise and the taps on the back but when you have the suit and have removed the risk of injury, the praise felt undeserved.

Normally I loved the contact and physicality of the game - being a bigger guy that was a big part of my game. But I pissed off the coach early on because while I was happy to finish my checks, I knew that with the suit, it added a bit of oomph to every check I gave. So when there was even a small chance that the check was late, I would pull out. That led to a few rough words on the bench from the coach and a chat after the game.

"What's going on out there?"

"Just learning what counts as a late check in the league, Coach. I didn't want to put us down a man if I got it wrong."

"Take the penalty. I want you to finish your checks."

"Got it Coach. Will do."

"Great game, keep it up!"

"Thanks!"

But being a star player was a bit of an adjustment for me. I looked around at the other players who led the team in salary. There was a deference to them in the locker room. The press certainly wanted to talk to them the most. Sure, they got the ice time and the pressure to perform. I knew that every season, they would be judged the most harshly by the pundits with their stats for the season compared with the salaries and grades discussed with solemnity. They also got the first go in the ice baths and the first dibs on the playlist in the locker room. They sat up the back in the bus or on the plane. They got the best stalls in the locker room.

But inside, I was still the big goof from the worst division in the beer league. In a beer league game, if a guy in our team had made three passes which had been picked off leading to goals and was feeling like absolute shit, I'd be talking to him about the play he made in the corner which had shut down a scoring opportunity. If a guy had ten shots on goal and missed every single one, then I'd be reminding him that he'd back checked every single time the other team had the puck. If there was a guy in the changing room with his head down, I'd shuffle over and check in on him. I didn't do this because I was a leader. I did it because I was a nice guy and knew how bad it felt to be given a hard time for being a weaker player. And when the game didn't matter, then this was an admirable quality.

I wasn't sure it would be as welcomed in the pro leagues when winning was the only thing that mattered. And it wasn't until the second month into my NHL career that I noticed that I was doing it again. It was being noticed by the coaching staff too. They didn't say anything but I could see them watching. So much for keeping a low profile and staying under the radar, huh?

Dead Man

Very early in the season, we had a practice open to the public. I barely noticed the crowd as I was focusing so hard on getting the drills right and doing what I needed to do. While in the games there is a visceral connection between on-ice events and the crowd's reaction, in an open practice nobody is applauding a particularly crisp pass or transition from the inside edge to outside edge while skating. So there was no reason to look up at the bleachers from the ice. But for whatever reason, I was waiting in line for my next turn at one of the drills and I idly scanned the stands.

I had started skating with my linemates in the drill before my brain caught up to what my eyes had seen and I momentarily faltered. I recovered and completed the drill before skating back to the end of the line, and then scanned the crowd again. Because the lizard part of my brain had registered that I had seen Seb, sitting in the crowd alone, watching me. He caught my eye and nodded. It was him. I stared back in disbelief. One of my teammates nudged me and I set off on the next iteration of the drill. Seb was alive? How was that possible? I completed the practice session in a daze, periodically checking that it was in fact him sitting there but trying hard not to just stand there and stare at him. I was tempted to just hold his gaze and skate over to the side of the ice and climb over the boards and walk up to him, so sure that he would dissolve into nothingness before I got to him. Trying hard not to believe my eyes, I wondered if this was the first sign of some sort of psychosis or if it was my mind dealing with the pressure of the stress and guilt of being in the team because of my suit.

I managed to get to the end of the session and instead of following the rest of the team to the changing rooms, I made my way to the side of the rink closest to where I had seen Seb. Seb made his way down to meet me, and I finally noticed that he wasn't alone - two men in black followed him down, stopping just out of earshot but scanning the crowd.

"We should talk," said Seb.

"You think?" I asked incredulously.

"Not here. Someplace quiet."

I gave him the name of a bar nearby and told him to give me twenty minutes. A quick shower later, I found him in the booth of the dive bar, noting that the two men in black were in a neighboring booth. Seb had got me a lager and was halfway through his already so I gathered he'd been there maybe ten minutes, waiting.

I raised the beer. "Here's to dead friends," I said and then took a long swallow.

He had the grace to look uncomfortable. "Yeah, I'm sorry about that, Phil. Sorry, Peter."

I waited, expectantly.

"I guess you've got questions."

"You think? What the hell happened? You died."

"Yeah, not my idea. You can thank me for the fact that you're still breathing too."

"You might have to explain that."

"Okay. So apparently, the feds had been watching the progress that Andrew had been making with the suit. They moved in pretty quick when it looked like he was going to sell it to foreign interests. They blew up the apartment to cover up our extraction. Kidnapping? Extraction. Anyways, they removed us to a lovely facility and then they finally figured out that the third man at the apartment wasn't you. They couldn't figure out what to do with me and I was pretty convinced that they were going to take advantage of the cover story of an explosion to permanently disappear me. You see, unlike you and Andrew, I hadn't done anything illegal. So they kept me on ice while they figured it out." He took a drink and then carried on.

"And then you popped up on the radar again with the suit fully operational. You see, they were incredibly interested in how you had done that - they apparently had come up against a brick wall in terms of programming their version of the suit. The tech that Andrew had put together to get the thing made in the first place was pretty close to what they had managed themselves, but getting it to the point of something usable had escaped them. Once they figured out that your suit had everything they needed, they planned to kill you and steal it but I managed to persuade them that if they removed the best player the NHL had ever seen, then there might just be a little bit of interest in how, why and who was involved with that. Maybe if someone close to you that you trusted offered to act as a go-between, then they would be able to get the tech that they wanted without attracting unwanted attention. So what do you reckon? If you can tell them about…" and here Seb turned his hand over to read something that had been scrawled on his palm in ballpoint pen, "…torsion mapping, whatever the hell that is, they will let you continue your career."

I blinked. This was a lot to take in. But I got the gist of it. If I was willing to share the products of my labor, then I got to live and to keep playing. A no brainer really. "Uh… one thing. What's to stop them from killing me anyway after I share the programming?"

Seb took a swallow of his beer before looking at me strangely. "Uh, the same reason they couldn't kill you before. You've got too much attention already. Keep up!"

I nodded, realizing I was being slow. "Oh, yeah. I get it now."

"No, I mean, keep up because it's your round." He waved the bartender over. "Look, they could have broken into the training facility and stolen the suit but that has risks and would only get them something built specifically for ice hockey. They're hoping that with your cooperation, they'll get something more generic which they can reprogram for whatever application is needed."

"And what application are they going to apply my programming to?"

Seb shot me a look over his newly arrived pint. "It's a bulletproof suit giving the person wearing it superhuman strength. What do you think that they want to use it for?"

The First Fight

The league may be constituted of a bunch of teams each made up of a number of players and coaches but it sometimes operates as a single organism. I'm not referring to the administration; more that it's like a collective consciousness made up of all the players on all the teams running on its own rules and ethics.

That organism watches all the rookies carefully and tests them to see if they're tough. Someone will take a run at them to see how they respond. And as a rookie, you're waiting for this and you steel yourself. You decide what you will do when that day comes.

I was suiting up for one of the early games and George, one of our older defenseman who had the stall next to me, turned to me as he wrapped sock tape around the top of his shin guards. "Do you think it will be tonight?"

I was baffled by what he meant. First goal? First check? "What do you mean? First what?"

"First fight."

"I'm not really a fighter."

"Yeh that's not quite how it works. Someone will probably take a run at you to see if you will stick up for yourself. Don't take it personally. It's just the league feeling you out. Just giving you a heads up."

"Thanks. It's not going to be their enforcer is it? I don't think I could take him on."

He laughed. "Nah, the point is not to beat you to a pulp. We'll look out for you. And who knows, they might see you out there and think that you're not a rookie. Maybe." He said the last with a smirk. One thing I was discovering was that there were no secrets. There were too many media outlets and fans with a penchant for stats and way too much time on their hands, not to mention the burgeoning sports data analytics firms starting up left and right.

But anyway, it wasn't long before I saw what he meant. One of our other rookies went into the corner to get the puck and one of their guys came swooping him and nailed him in the numbers. Definitely checking from behind. The rookie went down hard and then came up swinging. He had to let the league know that he wouldn't put up with that sort of nonsense. Sure, he got a five for fighting but anyone taking liberties would know that they should be invited to dance, there would be consequences.

The Forty Year Old Rookie

So I wasn't surprised when I was challenged in my next game. I was still playing fourth line minutes at that stage and the game was even. I think the guy that tapped my pads was a rookie looking for a fight to show that he could add value to their team - he wasn't going to make it as a skill guy, so hitting everything that moved, skating hard on the forecheck and dropping the mitts whenever possible were going to be his calling cards. The puck was in the neutral zone and two other players were competing for it against the boards and he was marking me. He started chirping me and then started whacking his stick on my pads. "Do you wanna go, old man? C'mon, let's dance."

I shrugged it off - on the fourth line, you don't get a lot of ice time, so the last thing I wanted was to spend time in the box instead of on the ice. But when I got back to the bench, the coach crouched behind me.

"What's the problem? Why didn't you want to fight? The team could have done with a boost."

I twisted to look at him. "You want me to fight?"

"Sure, unless there's a problem?"

"... uh no, no problem."

The next time I went out, we were lined up against a different line. Looking back on it now, I should have challenged one of those guys but for whatever reason, I was looking for the guy who had whacked me on the pads. Towards the end of the period, I got my chance. He gave me a tap and I nodded at him. We dropped our sticks and shook off our gloves. I had a couple of inches on him and tried to grab his right arm with my left hand but got a handful of sleeve instead. Still, it made it hard for him to get good punches going, and my extra reach made it hard for him to land anything good. For my part, I was having a hard time getting free with my right but I did manage a couple of shots but hit nothing but helmet. I'm not sure if those hurt him more than my fist but as I went to the penalty box, I noticed the referees had given me an extra penalty.

My suit had a partial glove for each hand which had sensors to allow me to stick handle and shoot, and that was connected to the rest of the suit at the wrist with a combination of a wire connector and a strip of Velcro. But the problem was that the part glove which covered the palm and wrapped around the index finger and thumb had been seen by the referees and they thought it was tape and that wasn't allowed. Or at least, it wasn't allowed for people fighting. I think originally it was to stop people from fighting with tape on their knuckles which would be more likely to cut the skin. It's the reason why boxers use Vaseline. A punch that slides off the skin is less likely to cut the skin, whereas anything like tape on the knuckles would be more likely to do more damage.

So, I ended up getting an additional penalty and a couple more minutes to think about things a little more. I was just glad to not disgrace myself with the fight. Well, I say fight but the armchair warriors online were less generous with their assessment. "Snore fest," "more of a cuddle than a wrestle," and "inconclusive," were the standouts.

But I realized that I might need to adjust my suit and maybe add some programming for the act of fighting, something which hadn't crossed my mind when setting it up originally. Fortunately, we had a day off the next day and so I sat in my apartment at my laptop, ingesting hockey fight videos and running algorithms to figure out the movements required and how they would be interpreted by the suit. I also made a modification so that the parts of the suit which covered the hand could be attached to the inside of the gloves and would come off when you took off the gloves. That took the whole day and I didn't have time to test it before the game the following night. I did have time to have a play with it during the warmup skate before the game and the switch around with the gloves didn't have too much of an impact on my stick handling or shooting. There were the obvious alignment issues where the suit glove wasn't sure which part of my hand was where but I had gone through that earlier and it was simple enough to give it a few lines of code to get the suit to detect the critical hand points and adjust its behavior accordingly. I made those changes just before my pregame nap, and felt good about it. But it would take a few weeks for it to come into use.

I had been put onto the second line and the extra ice time, plus being on the second power play line, was leading to a super noticeable increase in my point production. It was easier to get into a groove the more I played and the guys on my wings were more skilled and knew where they were supposed to be on the ice as well. Which is something I still struggled with. Again, it was my extra speed which made up for some bad decisions. Not that they led to turn overs or odd man breaks or anything like that - more that when we cycled the puck in deep, the coach's system was that we could roll out of the cycle with a pass to the point. As center, I should then be high in the slot and the wingers would be trying to screen the goalie but when our defenseman let the shot go, I was typically still deep in the corner. So instead of being in the right place to collect any loose pucks after either the opposing defenseman or the goalie blocked the shot, I was swinging up ice.

I got away with it because of a lucky bounce or two - the first time the shot grazed a defenseman and I ended up in the corner with it, totally fortuitously. The second time I was going fast enough to get to the puck after the goalie let out a big rebound and we started the cycle again. Anyway, it looked like I was doing well but I knew that the coaching staff would be spending some time with me at the next practice to get me more in sync with the system.

But I was scoring and so I was attracting attention from the opposition's players. Small things that players did to put you off your game. An elbow to the ribs in the corner. A slash on the laces as you go by, a slightly late check, that sort of thing. Most of them didn't matter to me because the suit took the impact and I felt very little. In fact, if I wasn't watching for them, I don't think I would have even noticed.

I played very physically. I finished every check and relished going into the dirty areas of the ice. It's very easy to say that when you have a suit protecting you from injury and heightened dexterity, but even when I was playing beer league, I would use my size to my advantage. Both giving and taking checks - I'd love it when I took the hit to make the play, and being larger spread the impact. I was very aware of the fact that it looked good to the rest of the team and the coach. I guess it also looked good for the fans but I tried as much as I could to ignore the cheers. If you start living by the fans' reaction, you would be devastated if they started to think less of you.

Anyways, I was getting a lot of attention from the opposition rat. That's the person who is normally not as skilled as others but is there to throw the star players off their game, and occasionally steps over the line to be a "dirty player". Some ignored that line and make it their goal to rile the opposition's skill guys up until they can't focus on their game. Like anyone playing that game, they usually back up their on-ice shenanigans with an above average fighting ability but they aren't a specialist fighter. They usually aren't the biggest guys on the ice which means they occasionally refuse to fight if they think that they're mismatched.

So a slash to the back of the calf (where the shin guards don't cover) later and I decided to let this guy know that I wasn't having any more of his shit, and slash his stick. I might have put a bit more into the action than I thought because the stick went flying. He came over and gave me a push and I asked him if he wanted to go. They were behind in the scoreboard and the chance for him to take out a second line player for the five minutes of penalty was enough incentive for him, even though I had three or four inches on him and at least twenty pounds. And this guy hadn't just been slashing at me but the other guys in the team as well.

So he dropped his gloves and I dropped my gloves and he grabbed for my jersey and got a good hold on my right arm. I tried to grab him and totally missed. My suit and all the science, coding and everything else still didn't make it a perfect system. I had a split second to realize what was happening before he hit me on the side of the head. I ducked my head behind my left shoulder and tried to swing my right fist, knowing that he had a good hold. I figured if I wasn't throwing punches, then at the very least I was twisting and moving around making me a harder target. My suit amplified the punch and he lost his grip, and I connected a glancing blow on his helmet. It was a hard punch, just misdirected, and twisted his helmet. It didn't go flying but it let him know the force behind each punch and I actually saw the recognition in his eyes as he realized what would happen if one of them landed.

He'd already got the outcome he was looking for - me off the ice for five minutes - so he went on the defensive and clinched in tight, holding my right arm with his left and my collar with his right, pulling my neck down. This had the effect of making it near impossible to get my right arm free for punches while freeing up my left. It also pulled me forward off balance a bit and was designed to drain my energy staying upright. So I started wailing away with my left hand on his ribs - the chest protection didn't cover that area very well and even though there wasn't much room to get good punches, the suit was magnifying the force and I was making good connection. I could feel his ribcage give a little with every punch and a grunt as it forced his breath out. After three or four punches, he got a better grip on me which stopped me swinging and the refs stepped in as it became apparent that he'd had enough. The last punch I got in resulted in a crunching sound which only registered when I was being led away by the linesman. As the linesman skated me to the penalty box and the crowd went wild, I tried to tell him that I thought I'd cracked the other player's ribs. The linesman couldn't hear me over the din and deposited me at the penalty box door. I was terrified that a broken rib would puncture the guy's lungs and cause bleeding. I had no medical training so I didn't know if that was possible and even if it was, would the adrenaline from the fight stop him from feeling how badly he'd been hurt? I couldn't take the risk, so instead of going into the penalty box, I did a turn and yelled at the lineman. He took the act as a show of rebellion at being sent to the box and turned to bodily get me off the ice. I let him guide me (a little roughly if I'm honest) to the box and huddled my head close to his.

"Tell the trainer to check his ribs!" I yelled.

He looked up at me. "What?"

"His ribs. I busted his ribs. Tell the trainer!" I said as I got into the box. There was a guy in a suit in the box with me but he was from the league and had a clipboard. I didn't think I was even supposed to talk to him, so he was no good to me. My combatant didn't go to the other penalty box and was instead leaving the ice straight away, which was a good sign, I hoped. I did see the linesman go over to the opposition bench and talk to the coaching staff there, so I was hopeful that the message gets through.

After the game, I got the guy's phone number from one of their trainers and sent him a text message. "Hey, hope you're not hurt too bad and hope to see you on the ice again soon 79". Sometime during the evening, he texted back: "Thanks man - busted ribs so out for a month at least. Thanks for telling the trainer."

Captaincy

It was still early in the season when I got approached by one of the assistant coaches. "Coach wants to see you, Peter."

Instantly mixed feelings. It could be a promotion to a higher line or it could be a special assignment for the next game. It might be shuffling players around. New wingers maybe?

Or it could be something I had done wrong. A demotion. Trying someone else on the power play. When a team was losing, it was normal to change things around but usually the only changes to a winning team were forced on the coach by injuries. And we were winning and I was playing well.

Coach was maybe ten years older than I was. He was tall and grizzled with a shock of snow-white hair. If you dyed my pre-NHL beard white, I could have passed for a disheveled super-sized Santa Claus but Coach was not much heavier than his playing weight, even twenty years after retiring. He had a reputation as a no-nonsense player back in his playing days, a solid two way forward who wasn't afraid to drop the mitts. As a coach, he had a certain way of doing things but he definitely wasn't someone whose door was always open, one of those 'let's talk about it' kind of guys.

The thing about beer league is that each team usually had a wife or girlfriend behind the bench who was there because the league regulations demanded a non-player have the title of coach/manager on the scoresheet. One of the senior players or the captain would normally take the drills should you decide to have practices that season. So having actual coaching staff was a bit of a novelty. All I knew was that Coach decided how much ice time I got, and which lines I skated on. So regardless of how good I thought I was or how well I played, it really didn't matter: he could bury my career. He could put me in positions where it was impossible for me to succeed. So I always showed him deference. Actually, I showed all the coaching and back-office staff deference but I watched for the coaches out of the corner of my eye and if I detected any negativity, I would spend more time with that coach and do my best to show that I was trying. Call it paranoia if you like. Or brown nosing, if you were being unkind.

"Ah, Peter, thanks for coming. Shut the door. Take a seat."

Oh shit, oh shit, oh shit. If he wanted the door closed, that was not a good sign.

"Two things. First thing is we're trying to make this team an environment of accountability where players are accountable for their performance on the ice. And we don't want you to be undermining that."

I blinked. This was a telling off. OK. "Cool, got it Coach. I was trying to boost team spirit but I'll be smarter with that."

"Good, good. The video guys are telling me that you're reacting well to their pointers."

"Yeah." I laughed. "But there are only so many ways you can answer the question of 'What were you thinking here?'"

He smiled along with me. Maybe I was off the hook. Was it just these two things?

"Also… uh… it's not unusual to have the best player on the ice be the captain and we've already selected our captain for the year."

"I don't want to be the captain."

"Hmm… he told me you threatened him."

"Threatened him? How?"

"He said that you threatened to break his nose and put him out of the lineup."

I paused. "Did he? Did he tell you why?"

"He said he was just hazing the rookies. It's a tradition. You have to pay your dues."

"Yeah, about that. Did he tell you who exactly he was hazing?"

There was an uncomfortable silence. He was losing control over the conversation.

"The rookies," he finally managed.

"Yeah," I said, leaning back in the chair. "Did he tell you what he was going to do?"

"I'm sure it was nothing."

"Maybe. I didn't think it was nothing. Here's what happened. He asked what I would do if he locked me in the restroom on the bus for an hour. I told him that I'd put him out of the lineup by breaking his nose. Then he asked what I would do if five of them put Stan in the toilet for an hour. I told him that I would put all five out of the lineup."

"And why would you do that? What's so special about Stan?"

"You've seen the burns on Stan's arms, right?"

"Yeah, he was in a car accident in juniors. Of course, that's sad but they weren't making fun of his scars. So?"

I leaned forward. "He was trapped in the wreckage of the car for an hour as the flames got closer and closer, so he's claustrophobic. Putting him in the toilet of the bus and trapping him there as a prank would be pretty close to psychological torture. So yes, I would break bones if someone did that." I paused and looked at

Coach for a second too long. "You and I get along, right? I know that you're the boss and you know that I want to play. You know that I don't want to be the player that the team revolves around. I don't talk to the GM and I don't undermine you as the coach. I keep my mouth shut in the room because this is your team."

The coach was watching me intently. I was saying the right things so far but he knew the other shoe would drop.

"But that's predicated on me respecting you. As a player, you've played a lot more games than I have. As a coach, you've probably forgotten more about hockey than I know. As a man…" I took a second to control myself. "Well, if you condone locking a claustrophobe in the restroom, then maybe I'm wrong about you as a man. And if I don't respect you, then all bets are off." I stood up and walked to the door, turning in the doorway. "Door open? Or closed?"

"Leave it open," he said.

I found a toilet and sat in the cubicle shaking. I had been so angry, I'd been a hair's breadth away from taking a swing at Coach. I had no knowledge of the career trajectory of people who had gotten into fist fights with their coaches but I would have bet a lot of money that the trajectory would have been a straight line downwards.

What had I been thinking? That wasn't the plan. The plan was to get Coach to trust me in any situation on the ice so then I got more ice time. More ice time, more points; more points, more wins; more wins, more chance of making the playoffs; more wins in the playoffs, more chances of winning the Cup. Simple plan. And I had put it all in jeopardy by getting in the face of my coach. For something that hadn't ended up happening. I put my career on the line for a hypothetical. What kind of moron did that make me?!

I walked around on tenterhooks for the next day and a half. I put a call into my agent.

"Peter, how are things going?"

"Uhhh… not good actually. I think I've stuffed up."

"Tell me what happened."

I told him what I had said and the background.

"Ah, I see. Well, I don't think you have anything to worry about."

"…Really? But I practically threatened him. Surely he'll take revenge? Won't he have to put me in my place?"

"Take a breath. First of all, your conversation happened in private, so there's no chance of his authority being undermined. Second of all, it sounds like he wasn't told the full story and thirdly, if he punishes you and the story comes out like you just told me, then he looks like a complete idiot, so I think you're going to be okay."

I didn't say anything because I was so relieved but he read that as me not believing him.

"And let's say that I'm wrong and you do get punished. What's he going to do? You just passed, what, thirty games played and just hit a hundred points? You've broken a ton of records. If he scratches you, the press will be up his ass asking why. He can't send you down to the AHL because you certainly don't need a conditioning stint and your performance is exemplary, so he can't demote you for that. Coaching you is so obvious that even my dog could do it: 'Collins? Play him more because he's scoring so much.' And this isn't the 80s, right? It's not like the Oilers where it doesn't matter if you score five because they will score nine and beat you. No, this league has much tighter defense. So your scoring is off the charts unusual and valuable. If he messes with that, he might get a call from the GM asking why. So just relax. You'll be fine. Anything else giving you heartburn? Saw you got your bonus for 20 games played. Did you buy yourself something nice?"

A couple of days later at practice, Coach pulled me to one side. "Hey, you know that thing we were talking about in my office? Don't worry about it - I sorted it."

The Forty Year Old Rookie

"Ah cool, thanks Coach." I didn't know what that meant. I didn't know what he had done. All I knew was that it was finished as far as he was concerned and that suited me just fine.

Christmas Presents

The Christmas break was a few days over the Christmas period where, if a player could get home and back in time for the next game, he could spend some quality time with family. It was much harder for the Europeans because by the time you'd flown home, it was pretty much time to turn around and fly back. Definitely better for the North Americans, although if you were from the wilderness away from airports, you might only just make it back for your next game.

I was in the changing room after a practice in late December when Karl, a grizzled veteran defenseman at the advanced age of thirty, came by. He'd been in the league forever and had originally come over from Sweden, so he still had a faint sing-song accent.

"What are you doing for Christmas?" he asked.

Playing computer games and eating a microwave meal for two all by myself was what I didn't say. "Uh... nothing at this point. Why's that?"

"Would you like to join me and my wife and kids for a home-cooked meal? We'll be having loganberries and stroganoff, and Kalen makes a delightful walnut loaf which you'd swear was actually meat."

"Oh, that would be lovely, thank you."

He texted me the address and said to come by just after lunch, and then headed over to talk to our Swedish rookie Mikael, I guessed to ask him the same thing. I didn't know if him inviting us was a team-initiated thing or just something he did off his own bat but it felt good to belong somewhere where the other players looked out for each other. Christmas could be a lonely time.

It had been a while since I had experienced a family Christmas and I didn't want to be a disappointing guest, so I texted Karl to see who else was coming in order to bring the right number of gifts. It was just going to be him, his wife and kids, and the rookie, so I went gift shopping.

On Christmas Day, I rocked up to their town house in the suburbs and rang the doorbell. His wife answered the door and invited me in. She was almost stereotypically Swedish, with blonde hair and bright blue eyes, and that lovely accent. I tried hard not to think about the Swedish Chef from The Muppets. I stopped off at the tree which dwarfed the lounge area and deposited my presents in the impressive pile underneath and then joined Karl in the kitchen where he was getting something out of the oven.

The afternoon whizzed by with a few beers and games with the kids. Erik was eight and Anders was five, and Mikael must have been brought up with siblings because he was right in there, playing knee hockey and battling away.

I had put some thought into their gifts and had some success. The kids were easy… well, easy if you had kids yourself. I had no idea but let myself be guided by the shop assistant in the toy department of the local department store. The internet had told me how old Karl's kids were, so I at least had got them something age appropriate.

Erik and Anders descended on the wrapped presents with their names on them. They smiled and thanked me for whatever was in them, and then they saw the envelopes for the adults. I had gotten Mikael an open flight home to Sweden.

The hosts laughed along when Mikael made the inevitable joke about trying to get rid of him, and I smiled too before cracking the next joke. That, if I really was trying to get rid of him, I'd be sending him to where our AHL or ECHL teams played instead of Sweden.

The hostess got a voucher for an hour at the local spa, which she seemed to appreciate and then Karl opened his. It was the smallest envelope and he mocked it gently by weighing it in his hand. But when he opened it, his eyes briefly filled with tears and he looked at it for a long time. His wife and kids came over to see what had affected him so much and looked incomprehensibly at what he held. Then his wife understood and her eyes filled with tears also.

"How did you know?"

It was a signed rookie card of the Swedish defenseman who had taken our veteran under his wing when he had come to the NHL. He had passed away the previous year and I had seen a photo of Karl at the funeral on his Wikipedia page. A little research had indicated that they had never played on the same team.

After dinner, we retired to the lounge and half watched an old black and white movie on TV. The kids had been told to call us Uncle Mikael and Uncle Pete as a sign of respect I guessed, and as we watched the movie, I could see Erik looking over at his two new uncles.

"Uncle Mikael, do you have a girlfriend?"

He colored. "Nobody steady yet. I'm playing the field."

I smiled.

"Uncle Pete, why don't you have a wife?"

"Well, that's a long story, kid. I did have a special someone a long time ago but things didn't work out."

"Did she leave you?"

"Erik!"

"No, she didn't leave me, she was taken away."

"Sorry about that. Erik, you can't ask questions like that."

"Why not? My teacher, Mr. Sears, at school, is old like Uncle Pete and his wife left him."

"Yes, but it's not polite to ask that question. It might make Uncle Pete sad."

Later in the evening, the kids had gone to bed but we stayed up. Karl looked like he wanted to say something but didn't quite know how to broach the subject. Eventually he said: "This is not a very Swedish thing to talk about, but do you mind talking about salary? Are you really only getting $2.25 million?"

A full belly and being nicely buzzed from the beers made me relaxed around financial questions. "With bonuses, yes."

"So you're better than Gretzky and he was paid what?" He grinned to show that he didn't necessarily mean the comparison.

"I don't think I'm better than Gretzky but you can't compare salaries that long ago. We've got the cap and he didn't, and that was the eighties, and this is now."

"You're breaking all the scoring records, so..."

"Yeah, but again the league is different now than it was when he was playing. So it makes the pay versus performance question difficult to answer."

"Do you know how much they'll be offering you?"

In the NHL, the team you were under contract with could offer you an extension from the 1st of January of the last year in your contract. Most teams that wanted you to play for them long-term would sign you to an extension before you hit the open market at the end of the contract on the 1st of July. The length of the extension for me would only ever be one year because of my age. I shook my head and smiled. "Well, the top salary in the league is currently $13M, so I guess they'll offer that."

He looked at me. "Sooo… that particular top salary was gotten two years ago, and the only reason it hasn't moved is because none of the top players have had to renegotiate their deals for a couple of years. And in those two years, the salary cap has gone up, so the top salary as a percentage of the total cap would be much higher now than it was two years ago."

I must have looked confused.

"Look, let's use nice round numbers so then the math is easy, okay?"

I nodded.

"You're the best player in the league, right. So two years ago, let's say that the cap, that's the total of all salaries for the team, is say $90M. The top salary of all players is $13M. So as a percentage, the top guy is getting paid..." - he typed some numbers into his phone - "14.4% of the team's cap. So if the top guy is paid 14.4% of the cap and the cap goes up to $100M - and again these are nice round numbers - then you would expect the top guy to get $14.4M. Now that's based on comps - the salary that players who are comparative to you are getting. But if you make the argument that you're better than the guy who's getting paid the most, then your agent would be looking at trying to get more than that percentage."

"What, like 20%?"

He laughed out loud. "Leave some money for the rest of us! You might find a team somewhere who are rebuilding who would pay that to one player but no, I don't think any GM will give you that much. You could argue for 15%, that would probably be agreed to. But think about it. If you got, say, 16%, then you would be getting about one sixth of the cap and the GM would have only five sixths of the cap to find a way to pay nineteen or twenty other players. Now that's not your problem. Talent needs to be paid. And there's only so much talent in the universe, right? But what's your deal now? Two? Two and a quarter? You'll be looking at more than a $10M raise. Merry Christmas!"

I was a bit stunned as the reality of what he was saying sunk in. If I kept half of what I earned after agent fees, state taxes in every city I played in, and then federal taxes on top, then my very comfortable current salary would very shortly be a rather steep upgrade to the kind of things you'd see in a 'Lifestyles of the Rich and Famous' program on TV. And I would have to do everything in my power to make sure that it didn't end up being one of those ones where the rich person loses it all to bad investments, bad advice and untrustworthy advisors.

I thanked my hosts and headed back home by taxi, smiling as Kalen put a blanket over Mikael who had fallen asleep on the couch in front of the TV.

Then in the new year, my agent gave me a ring.

"Are you sitting down? The GM just got off the phone to me. They want to extend you for next season. They're willing to offer you $13M. I told them they're dreaming and that if they want the best guy in the league, then they should be offering the best money. I think we should go back at $15.5M. I can probably get a lot of it up front."

"Up front?"

"Yeah, as a signing bonus. That makes it guaranteed money in case of a lockout or injury."

"I thought they would be trying to minimize their risk?"

"Oh, I'll ask for all of it up front and settle for as much as they'll let us. It's a negotiating tactic. You ask for the stars and settle for the moon."

"That's a lot of money... Who would we lose if they agreed to that? Probably Gordo, Perrin and AJ, right?"

"And Lebroski as well. They would need to give Fyodr and Alex a raise and then you have your bonus rollover from this year. They would then have to find four players at $1m each for the next season but they can start working on that now."

"I kind of like Gordo and AJ. They seem genuinely friendly."

"Well, they can't magic money out of nothing. Do you want to take a pay cut so then they can keep them?" He guffawed like that was idiocy.

"Can we do that?"

There was a pause as he considered how to answer that question. "We can do anything you want." I quickly did the math. I figured 3% of $10m was $300k, so every $1m we came down was $30k out of his pocket. So even though he would personally financially lose on the proposed deal, if it made me happy, then he would try to get it done. Sometimes it wasn't about getting the most money, or the longest deal, or the best signing bonus.

"Can we put that in the contract?"

"It's not one of the standard clauses. And even if we could, it's not enforceable. Nobody will handcuff themselves with something like that. What if you get injured and then not only do they not have you on the ice but they also no longer have the flexibility to make the team better because they have agreed to lock in those players. But if I explain that you're willing to take a hometown discount because you like playing with those particular players, I think that he'll respect it. They'll want you to be happy and star players always get a say in personnel. Just look at Jagr at the Rangers. It was a Czech show. And Messier in Vancouver. He had a lot to say about the roster."

I frowned down the phone. Sure, Jagr had success with his countrymen in New York, but Messier in Vancouver? Hadn't I watched a video on YouTube where they said that he single-handedly ruined the franchise for a decade with his demands? Did I want that much control? I mean, sure, the suit allowed me to play really well but how did that equate to having insight into what would make the team great? How did that relate to knowing which players to get and which to trade away?

"But here's the thing," he continued. "If we drop the amount we're asking for, you're actually screwing over the guys that come after you. Because if you're the second-best player in the league and your contract comes up for renewal, the GM will point at your contract and tell the player that he's not as good as you so why should he be paid as well? You're artificially depressing the price for top end talent. There are players that are overpaid. Then there are players who are paid fairly. Then there are players who are on team-friendly deals. If we lower the price we ask for you by too much, then we will be inventing a totally new category. I'll see what options are on the table."

Pressed by the Press

The press were funny. Some of them couldn't get their heads around the fact that I wasn't going to talk about my past. And compared with everyone else in the league, whose history was a matter of public record with their stats from every league that they had played in, I certainly stood out in that regard. Maybe if I was a fringe player just getting a look into the first team that would have been less of a story but I was putting up pretty impressive numbers. Which meant that the questions would pop up again and again.

"Where did you play last season?"

"I'm sorry, I'm not going to talk about that."

It helped a little that I was thoughtful and, I hoped, insightful about the game. I was certainly respectful of my teammates, the coach, the opposition and the league. The last thing I wanted to do was to say the wrong thing. Normally that would make the answers to questions very vanilla and boring. When you know that everyone wants you to say something that they can blow out of proportion, you learn pretty quickly to be guarded and not to say anything which might lead to a pissed-off teammate, a reduction in ice time or a fine from the league. But even if I didn't want to answer particular questions, I always made sure I had something to add and hopefully something that the reporter could run with and put their own spin on.

"You've had a fantastic start. You must be happy with that?"

"I've been working with the coaching staff learning the system and adjusting to the pace of the league, and that's really paying dividends."

"You're the highest scoring rookie this season and if you keep up this pace, you are projected to score over two hundred points, that must be a satisfying feeling?"

"Well, I'm not a rookie officially, am I? It's my first season though, so I take your point. But I'm not worried about the personal stats, I'm more interested in learning the game and contributing in all parts of the ice. There's no point in two hundred points if you don't make the playoffs, right?"

"But two hundred points would be an impressive season surely? Nobody has scored that many since Wayne Gretzky."

"Yeah but Wayne played in the snatch and grab era. Elbows flying everywhere. If they had as much space as we've got now, who knows what he would have done. It's dangerous comparing eras."

Afterwards, I chatted with one of the other reporters and dropped a nice juicy quote which I knew would top his story. "I'd rather be a two-hundred-foot player than a two-hundred-point player." The next day: "Collins: 200ft > 200pts."

I read all the articles written after that interview. One was full of analysis of how many points were equivalent in each era and where each player stacked up based on that era's average goals per game. One wrote about the most impressive rookie seasons and where mine was in comparison. I knew that if my performance dropped then they would be the first to be in my face about it but until then, the sharks were placid.

Even after the local press got it in their heads that I wouldn't be answering questions about my history, the success we had as the season went on attracted more and more attention. There would be a scrum in the locker room after every game and the knot around my stall would be more and more densely packed with reporters. I was bewildered by the attention and would get confused as to which reporter had asked the question, often getting caught on the camera twitching to the left and then the right as I tried to focus on who had spoken. It would be easy to say that professional athletes shouldn't read what was written about them but that's just not realistic. There's a public discourse about the team that is triggered by articles and news stories, and then continued in the comments underneath them online. The only advice I was given was to avoid reading those comments as that was where the real poison was. That didn't stop some reporters from doing hatchet jobs though. I guess when you're writing about the team day in and day out, you need to find some unique point of view and having a middle of the road opinion doesn't bring eyeballs.

As a fan, I had watched the testy responses that some pros had given reporters in the scrum but I knew that I probably wasn't smart enough or quick enough to quip in the heat of the moment. But the things that I did learn pretty quickly were to say things like "I reject the premise of your question." That one really shut down some of the more pressing questions. Another was "I don't need to answer that one." But one thing that really got the sand in the machine was when we weren't playing well. I was lucky during the season that we only had one or two skids where we lost more than a couple of games in a row. When that sort of thing happens, you get critical articles written about you and then you read them and it's possible to take the criticism to heart. Taking careful note of which author's name was on the byline was important. The longer the losing streak, the more the reporter took apart what they thought was wrong with the team or focused on the players causing the losses, and then you got a really testy relationship. As I say, we were lucky the team stayed buoyant and upbeat through most of the season. But there was one reporter who always tried to be a hard ass.

"Peter, Gary Kopeka, The Daily News. The team has slumped to a three-game winless streak, what's gone wrong?"

"Gary, have you been watching the games? We had a blowout loss tonight which was probably helped by being the second in a back-to-back, home and home, straight after a long road trip. We did alright on that ten-day road trip but those miles add up. I don't think we had a bad game last night. I think we got some unlucky bounces and it really could have gone either way. So it's way too early to start panicking or to start looking for things that need changing. We're not going to win every single game. I mean, we're going to try to win every single one but sometimes that's not going to happen. And that's good because we'll learn something when we lose. It might be something about ourselves and Coach will make a tweak or address an issue. Or it might be something we learn about the opponent. And Coach will squirrel that away for the next time we play them or more importantly, for the playoffs."

The press had so many inches of column to fill, so many words they had to file every day, that sometimes their stories weren't just wrong opinions, they were just bizarre. Admittedly it wasn't necessarily the beat writers that had the strange questions, it was more likely to be the non-hockey outlets who resorted to the most nonsensical questions. "What animal would you be?" "What pancake would you be?" "Would you rather fight a duck-sized horse or a horse-sized duck?" That sort of thing.

It was tempting to treat those questions with the contempt that they deserved but after I thought about it, what would that achieve? It would make it harder for the writer to put together their story and tick that off their list of things that they had to do. On the one hand, it would show that I did not suffer fools gladly but on the other, it would show that I was an asshole and would not entertain playful exchanges. What would I really gain? My time had already been wasted by listening to the question!

Periodically there would be a story in the press with someone who claimed to know Peter Collins from back in the day and sometimes they did and sometimes they didn't. Either way, I would neither confirm nor deny the story and so there was quite the collection of possible histories for readers to choose from. I even muddied the waters further by making changes to my Wikipedia page, implying that I had been in prison for ten years. I figured that would satisfy some people who really wanted to know my personal history, while also providing a reason for my reluctance to talk about it.

Not long after I did that, the press got wind of it and I got a bunch of questions about it. Of course, I told the reporters the same thing that I had been telling them all season, that I wouldn't be commenting on it. One guy wouldn't let it go.

"If you were an ex-convict, it would be a great opportunity for you to tell your side of the story and show that convicts can be rehabilitated into society."

I held his gaze steadily and said, "If."

He got uncomfortable and tried a different tack. "But if you were in prison for a long time, wouldn't you want to tell your story?"

I shook my head. "If, and I stress, if I was in prison for a long time, then that stint in prison would be because I did something wrong. And if that was the case, then that stint in prison would be payment for whatever I did wrong, right? So nobody, not you, not the league, not society at large, would have any claim to know what

I had done because that debt to society had been paid and forgiven.... if I had been in prison."

"Surely we have a right to know your backstory?"

"More of a prurient interest, maybe. But no, not a right to know."

The people I felt a little sorry for were the people that I had actually worked with ten or more years ago. This was way before working from home was so prevalent but that meant that they only had blurry non-digital photos of someone in a badly fitting suit who was tall and thin and looked somewhat like me, or else not even that - just the recollection that someone on a Zoom call five years ago had looked a little bit like Peter Collins but back then, he had gone by the name of Phil Collins. The name change did wonders for putting people off the scent. In fact, there was a growing group of conspiracy theorists who had come up with various entertaining and intricate reasons why this or that person who vaguely resembled me were, in fact, me. They kept the speculation of my background in the realm of the crazy or deluded rather than giving credence to any of the theories that were actually close to the truth.

When you're living guiltily and you don't get found out for a while, your sensitivity to the hand on the shoulder diminishes but never goes away. I think that the natural reaction to being found out is one of shock but then one of relief as you can finally relax and the worst has happened. As the season went by, the tension I felt about potentially having my suit found out diminished a little, which is why when my other secret came out, it was so devastating.

It happened in a press conference following my achievement of a particular milestone, I think it was fifty goals in the fewest games in league history. I had fielded the usual questions about how it felt, giving due credit to my teammates ("You can't score that many goals without getting great passes from your team") and the coach ("If I'm not on the ice, I can't score") when someone at the back of the room asked a question I had not been expecting.

"Were your parents Randy and Jenny Collins?"

My jaw hung open for a few seconds.

"And were you engaged to Katie Turner?"

My eyes began to water. The media manager looked very confused, looking back and forth between the journalist asking the question and where me and Coach were sitting on the stage.

"Yes. What's your question?"

The journalist blinked in surprise. They obviously hadn't trusted their source and now had confirmation that it was true.

"Uh... when was the last time you visited their graves?"

The room turned icy and the journalist found himself on the end of some nasty looks and a general rumbling of discontent came from the other journalists. I don't know how much of that came from being scooped and having the confirmation presented right in front of them, and how much was a reaction to a deeply inappropriate question, but all of a sudden, they didn't have many friends in the room.

"Do you have any hockey-related questions?" The media manager had stepped in, asserting control of the room. "No? Then we will move on." She selected one of the other media outlets for the next question and the press conference continued. But my heart wasn't in it. My answers began to get shorter and the Media Manager noticed that. Instead of a half hour, she pulled the plug after only half of that.

Coach asked me if I was okay on the way out.

"It was fifteen years ago, Coach. I should be okay. But sometimes it's like it was yesterday. It hurts, you know?"

He gave me the sympathetic half smile of someone who hasn't lost anyone close to them yet and we kept walking. When the story of their accident broke the next day, they didn't mention the fact that my parents had been driving my fiancé back from the clinic and they didn't mention the Bump.

The Last Fight

I was picking up a lot of points and had moved up both in terms of which line I was on and the role I was expected to play. Instead of being on the fourth line, expected to chase hard on the forecheck and be a high energy guy, I was now on the first line and was expected to score. My linemates were more skilled than when I was on the checking line and my ice time went through the roof. I was going from six or seven minutes per game to fifteen or sixteen. I didn't care which of those was driving the point production, I was just enjoying getting the puck in the back of the opposition's net and keeping it out of ours. That increase in points was noticed by our opposition and I noticed a change in their approach to countering me in turn.

I started to get a lot more challenges to fight. Niggly little plays started to become more commonplace – cross-checks, slashing and scrums with a little more extracurricular activities designed, I was sure, to get me off my game and encourage me to get in a fight. If I was off the ice in the penalty box, then I couldn't score. It made sense.

I had a word with Coach about it.

"Hey, do you want me to fight out there?"

"You can't play if you break your hand on someone's helmet. Let Tony take care of it."

I nodded and for a while, my response to a cross-check and an invitation from an opponent would be, "Sorry, Coach says I can't."

Tony certainly stepped up when he could but there were plenty of tough guys on the other side who wanted to be the guy that got me off the ice, so in the end, we used the media to get people off my back. In one of the post-game press conferences, Coach explained that he'd had a word with me and that going forward, he was banning me from fighting and he'd bench me if I did. It was a statement to the rest of the league that I wasn't going to be dropping the gloves and to stop asking.

I started to feel more confident on the ice and even started to be in the right place at the right time. The one-to-one sessions with the coaching staff finally making the coach's system stick. We were facing an interdivisional rival and the game was a very tight affair. They were doing a good job of marking me and even with my superior pace and mobility, I was not really able to dominate. Their goalie was having an outstanding game as well. I was playing first line by this time and starting to really feel secure in my spot on the roster. After the coach had made the announcement about fighting, I wasn't being constantly hassled by every young guy trying to make his name in the league and that allowed me to really focus on my game. It was halfway through the second period when the puck was deep in our zone along the boards and a scrum of six players were trying to dig it out. The opposition took the opportunity to grab a change and for whatever reason, their defensemen came charging down the boards and nailed our winger in the numbers. He was pretty close to the boards but hadn't seen the guy coming and of course, hadn't expected the force of a half-ice sprint straight into him and so hadn't been bracing himself. Naturally, he went face first into the glass, and then crumpled on the ice.

Everyone on the bench was on their feet, protesting the injustice. On the ice, a scrum formed around the offending player, with everyone trying to get to him, their other players getting in the way, and lots of shoving, pushing and jawing. I'm pretty sure someone would have challenged him to fight but he wasn't interested. It got heated and the refs took a while to get everything under control.

Our guy came off under his own steam but as soon as he was off the ice, he was helped by the trainer and headed down the tunnel.

C. G. Lambert

We ended up with an extra two-minute power play. Coach came over and tapped my line for the start of the power play but I told him that I was gassed and we'd go out second, if that was alright with him. He glanced at me sideways but nodded and put out the second unit. They got some looks but as I said, the opposition goalie was standing on his head. The second unit stayed out a little long and we were looking at less than a minute left in the penalty. I felt frustrated that the miscreant hadn't been given a major for boarding, intent to injure or even a double minor for roughing and so when we went over the boards for the change, I decided to do something about it.

We had control of the puck in their zone and were moving the puck around the periphery, looking for an opening. There were ten seconds left in the penalty and so I skated over to the penalty box and waited, staring at the guy who had done the boarding. His teammate who was in for his own two-minute roughing penalty looked over at me and quickly looked away. As the penalty expired, the gate opened and out came the perpetrator, heading for their benches. He hadn't clocked me yet but when his mate called out to him to watch out, he looked up and realized that I was going to fight him no matter what he did and he grinned. I saw red. I had my gloves off in an instant and grabbed him. To his credit, he dropped his stick and gloves as well, reaching out to grab my jersey to stop me from getting a punch away. He was successful in grabbing my arm but I managed to get a hold of the collar of his shirt and pulled down with my left hand while planting an upper cut on his chin. I had pulled him off balance and he was tipped forward so I really caught him flush. I didn't notice that he wasn't holding onto my arm so it was a free hit with the suit. I felt something give and he went down in a heap. I was already over by the penalty boxes, so I opened the door and took a seat. It had not taken long at all.

The trainer had to come out to help my combatant off the ice and it took a few minutes for them to clear away the blood. I watched this all from my vantage point in the penalty box but by the time play was to resume, the refs sent me to the changing rooms instead. I had a five-minute penalty and there was less than five minutes to go in the period, so there was no point in me being in the box. I think the refs were more worried that constantly seeing me in the box would antagonize the other team and make them want to exact revenge.

When the team joined me in the changing room between periods, Coach came over and had a quiet word.

"How's the hand?"

"It's good, thanks. I caught him flush."

He looked uncomfortable. "Hey, you know how we spoke about getting in fights…"

I nodded. "It might be a good idea to bench me for the third."

He looked relieved. "Yeah." He strode over to the middle of the room and gave his brief talk about what we had been doing well and what we needed to work on for the third period and then headed back out.

As soon as he left, a little knot of players formed around me.

"Man, you really did a number on him. I saw him as he was helped off the ice. His nose was spread over his face. It was a real bloody mess."

"Remind me not to piss you off, dude!"

I smiled modestly. Protecting your teammates was a valuable currency. Tony, our enforcer, came over.

"Hey, stick to your own thing, man. I was going to get him on my next shift."

"Yeah, sorry Tony. My bad. Coach is going to bench me for it. I should have let you sort it." I think I did a good enough job of selling my contrition because he nodded and strode away, having made his point.

Coach only ended up benching me for half the third period and by the end of the game, we'd gotten two past their goalie to take the win. I had gotten an empty net goal and so had come close to getting a 'Gordie Howe hat trick', which was when instead of scoring three goals in a normal hat trick, you got a goal, an assist and a fight.

Our guy who had been run over was okay in the end and was back in the room talking about the replays of my fight making the highlight reel. He wasn't the only one who had seen the results. The footage from the game was particularly graphic and the websites who focused on fighting had to put an advisory warning on the videos. In the media scrum after the game, of course, the only thing people wanted to talk about was the fight.

"Look, Coach made it very clear what would happen if I got into another fight. He quite naturally doesn't want me to break a bone in my hand punching someone, causing me to miss game time. I went against that and fully respect whatever punishment he hands down."

"What do you say to people that say you shouldn't scratch your star player? That you're needed on the ice?"

"I'd say, you don't understand who's in charge here. This is Coach's team and he sets the rules. It's the same if I come back from drinking after curfew or if I don't play the right way."

"You really nailed him. Have you been practicing fighting?"

"I knew that getting into a fight would have consequences for me but I wanted to make sure that he knew that there are consequences for his actions too."

The pantomime of Coach telling me in public not to get in any more fights was a welcome relief. While I felt there was no real physical danger to me getting into fights because of the suit (and it was much later that I realized that even with the super strength and technique, fights being what they were, it was totally possible to get hurt through a fluke punch or an unlucky fall), by being told not to fight, I no longer felt like I had to be the judge and jury of what constituted acceptable play on the ice. If Coach hadn't told me to keep my gloves on, then after every hit on the ice, I would have to determine whether it was a late hit or not. Every trip would have to be scrutinized to see whether it was knee-on-knee or not. I would be analyzing every action on the ice to determine whether retaliation was justified or not.

Regardless of what I thought, there would be Coach pointing to the opposing player and saying 'get that guy.' So I would not even be able to act according to my own conscience. Because if you're deemed a fighter and you don't fight on the command of your Coach, then even if you're contributing with points or defensive responsibility, you're not the tool the Coach wants and so they'll find another one.

If my only skill was fighting, then I would be off the team very quickly. I just wasn't built that way, to seek out confrontation on the ice. I would tell myself that it was because I was a nice guy but the events over that season made me seriously reconsider how true that really was.

'Stolen valor' is when someone tells people that he is or was a member of the armed forces when they weren't. They attempt to get the kudos of having served their country without the actual commitment, ability or being put in harm's way. They inevitably choose a cool branch of the military as their phantom service - nobody ever falsely claims to have served in the motor pool, right? It's a terrible thing to do because you've done nothing to earn it.

Every now and again, I would find myself looking around at an arena that I had watched a million times on TV and I would see it from ice level, while playing against players I had read about and watched a million times and I would pinch myself with glee. *I was doing this!*

That would be followed pretty swiftly by feelings of guilt. For two reasons. The first was that the suit was the only thing that had got me into the league. Obviously. The second was a bit more insidious. Every shot I took, every check I made, every takeaway, and every pass were all because of the suit. So the congratulations of my team members after a goal or a pass felt hollow, not because they didn't wholeheartedly mean them, but because they weren't congratulating me, it was my suit. The roar from the crowd when I blocked a shot, the excited commentary from the announcers when I sprinted back to break up a two-on-one; they weren't the result of having a team-first attitude and wanting to protect the goalie from an A-grade scoring chance. It was from the knowledge that I wouldn't be hurt. Breaking up the two-on-one didn't show responsible team defense. It was because getting back, even when tired, was less of an imposition than double tapping the W key on a keyboard to sprint in an NHL computer game.

Whenever I was faced with my self-image as a good guy and the reality of what I was doing and the stage I was doing it on, I would have to say to myself, "Would anyone turn this down? Would they? Really?" When I rhetorically asked myself who I was robbing and

The Forty Year Old Rookie

who I was wronging, I would sit silently and eventually admit to myself that I was robbing everybody. I was robbing the game of an honest competition.

The Reviews

They tell everyone not to read reviews. Authors, actors, musicians and especially athletes. Think about it. Whatever your opinion about something artistic, you can justify it and discuss and debate it, and you can agree or disagree with someone else's opinion. But there is no objectivity. It basically comes down to whether you like something or not. But athletes? Sure, you can like or dislike a player and you can have an opinion on their style of play and how well they do their job, but the numbers are the numbers. If you're on the team to score goals and you're not scoring, then there is no hiding from that fact.

Then there are those on the fringes; the trolls who say poisonous, hateful and hurtful things just because they don't know or don't care that there's a human being behind the song, the performance or the book that they've read. So they spew bile and say things that would get them punched in the mouth if they said it in person, and hide behind their keyboards and VPNs and anonymized IP addresses.

Some of the things written about me early on were that I was soft. That was usually after I passed up a chance to check someone because I was still learning what constituted a late hit in the league. So after a while, I was finishing my checks along with everyone else but there were some that still parroted the opinion as if I wasn't throwing any checks at all. I felt like asking them if any of the guys I obliterated in fights thought I was soft. The guy who needed cosmetic surgery to reconstruct his nose probably didn't think so.

But the most frustrating things to read were the comments about my points performance. I was breaking records left and right but if I scored more goals than assists in a game, then I was selfish and not passing enough. But if I got more assists than goals, then I was gun shy and should shoot more. My shooting percentage was high compared to the rest of the league, which led to some commenting that it was unsustainable and would revert to a more normal percentage, so my current performance was an anomaly.

God forbid I should have a game where I scored fewer than three points. The knives would come out then. Getting on the scoreboard of an NHL game in any capacity was an achievement. But not for some commentators. It showed that I wasn't trying and that I had taken my foot off the gas. The more perceptive of the trolls would complain that I wasn't able to shake the heavy marking of the opposition or adjust my game to having less time and space. That was a shortcoming of my game.

Now the normal way of judging a successful regular season is if your team makes the playoffs. Some teams are expected to go deep into the playoffs but to achieve this, they have to first make the playoffs. That's the only thing that matters. When you have as strong a season as we were having, you have to defend yourself from what I ended up calling 'the 100%ers.' Those were the critics who thought that we should win every single game in the regular season.

Then there were those who realized that maybe you wouldn't win every single game but because you were pretty much guaranteed to make the playoffs, that some other arbitrary target should be achieved instead. Like we had to win a certain number of games because a particular team in history had won that many games.

It was a strange situation that loving the game meant that you had to stay away from the people who were the most passionate about sharing their opinions on it.

Speaking of reviews and negativity, this is how petty it got. We had gone into a game with the usual number of players: twelve forwards, six defenseman and two goalies. But early on, one of the defensemen got injured and then another one went down later in the period. Finally, at the beginning of the second period, one of the other defensemen got a bit banged up and all of a sudden, we didn't have two lines of defensemen. Coach looked around and his eyes lit up when he saw me. By that stage, we were up 4-1 and pretty much in control. Coach comes over and asks if I had ever played D. I looked up at him and lied and said no. He said he'd try me there and I shuffled down the bench to join my new linemate. He had to shuffle the forward lines a bit and while he did that, the defense coach came up to me and gave me some advice.

"Concentrate on your gap - the distance between the puck carrier and yourself, and angle them to the boards."

I nodded as I understood that now the shoe was on the other foot - all the moves I had been doing on the poor defensemen in the league would now be visited upon me. I would need to really concentrate on my speed. It was no longer a tool to get me out of trouble when I screwed something up by not being in the right place at the right time or a tool to chase down odd man rushes and break up an opponents' offensive opportunities.

Now it was a dangerous tool because if I went too fast backwards while defending, the gap between myself and the puck carrier would be too large and he would have too much space to make a move or take a shot. If I slowed down too much, then the puck carrier could put on a burst of acceleration and go right past me before I could react and alter my speed. Angling was all about getting the puck carrier to go around me on the side closest to the boards so then I could deny him the middle of the ice where the shooting would be more lucrative for him. I could take him to the boards and he had only half as much room to try and dodge my check.

I quickly learned how to leverage my superior speed. Normally, a forward would have the puck and be approaching you. They'd chip the puck past you, and then try and get past you themselves to pick up the puck, before you could catch up with them. So normally, the defenseman would try and get in their way as they skated by. Not too much, otherwise you'd be called for interference. But enough to slow them down. I figured out that I could turn and match their speed, so instead of having to try and slow them down by skating in their path, I would take a different approach and time my skating to arrive at the puck a split second after they did, landing an enormous hit on the forward the second his stick touched the puck. I nailed three of their forwards this way before their coach changed tactics and instead of dumping the puck into the corner and chasing it, they just dumped the puck into the corner and went for a change.

I screwed up a couple of times figuring out whether I was supposed to be in front of the net marking a player or picking up someone else, but me playing defense worked out okay for the rest of the game. In fact, I had more ice time than normal because I was on the ice for half of the rest of the game. I was able to react to the changes in speed of the opponent puck carriers and anticipated their moves when they were trying to get past me. When we had the puck, I was able to keep the puck in their zone and jump into the cycle and keep the pressure on them. We had shifts where the forwards changed three times and we just kept cycling the puck and keeping it in their zone. When I got too excited and joined the cycling, one of the forwards would cover for me at the point and then I'd swap back. It was great time and I was very productive with another four points as a defenseman, all assists, for a five-point game in a very one-sided win.

You know what some schmuck online said? He said that I had demanded to play defense because I not only wanted all the scoring trophies as a forward but that I also wanted to get the Norris trophy as the best defenseman in the league. Of course, that's not mentioning the other positional trophies that I was equally not eligible for - coach, GM, and goalie. I guess it boiled down to this - nobody would be happy with my performance. Sorry, no. That's not right. There would always be someone who wasn't happy with my performance. If I was looking for universal acclaim, then sure, I would be as close to that as anyone would be but that would still never be 100%. It was only human nature for the negativity of that small number of discontented people to overwhelm the positivity of the vast majority.

It wasn't only the press and public that could be dissatisfied with players, and it sometimes came with a monetary penalty. The All-Star Game was a tradition where the regular season would pause for a few days and the best players, however that was decided (because the method for choosing the players changed periodically), would play a special mini tournament with the winning team having a million dollars donated to the charity of their choosing. The day before the games, there would be a skills competition among the players in the All-Star Game, with the first prize being another cool $1M.

Now, for most of the other players attending, a million was a lot of money but not as much proportionally as it was for me. Most of

The Forty Year Old Rookie

the other star players were on $5M+ so it was like, if I win this competition, then it would be a 20% bonus. For me, it was closer to a 50% bonus, so it was a bigger deal.

The league really hates it if the players it chooses decide that they would prefer to use those days for resting their body. Especially the slightly older players. When that happened, the league would actually fine the player selected if they didn't show up. It was okay if a player was injured and couldn't attend - they would be replaced by the next player in the list. But there was a weird seriousness around the All-Star Game. Like it didn't matter but it did matter.

And so I found myself on a Friday night in February warming up for a bunch of skill tests against the best hockey players in the world with a million dollars on the line. I took warming up very seriously because the only thing worse than potentially failing in an embarrassing way would be to hurt myself or someone else. Oh, and did I mention this was in a full arena and televised?

The best part was selecting which events I wanted to compete in. Every year, there's a different format. This year, they had got twelve players, made them choose four events each out of a list of six, and then the top eight performers did another event and then finally the top six went head-to-head in the last event. So out of

C. G. Lambert

Fastest Skater, Hardest Shot, Stick Handling, One Timers, Passing Challenge, and Accuracy Shooting, I selected Fastest Skating, Hardest Shot, Stick Handling and the Passing Challenge. You'd think with my abilities that I might have chosen the One Timer or Accuracy Shooting but those events required someone else feeding you the puck and I was very interested in that prize money, so I didn't want to be at the mercy of someone else's errant pass or slow reactions.

Needless to say, the Fastest Skater was in the bag as long as I didn't take a tumble. I managed to get around in less than thirteen seconds, beating the next best by half a second. The Hardest Shot was another open and closed case - I managed to nail my second shot and hit 105mph. Not the hardest ever recorded but the best of the class. Stick Handling was a sleepwalk for me with the suit doing all the hard work. All of the other participants struggled with the Passing Challenge because in every on-ice situation, the recipient of the pass is in motion, so you're used to leading the man and passing the puck to where the receiver is going to be. Or maybe where he should be. In either case, the other participants had mixed success altering their mentality while I was nailing the small targets left and right.

I wasn't sure what to expect for the first event in the second round after making the cut - it was a series of one-on-ones with the goalie, and on paper, I thought I would be unbeatable. But then I realized that in a game, getting a one-on-one with the goalie happened rarely and when it did, you were warmed up and you had some game time with the puck on your stick and your head was where it needed to be to maximize your chances of scoring. With the one-on-one challenge, you skated back and forth doing as many shootouts as you could in a minute. I must admit that the first five shots, which had to be taken below the hash marks, were saved pretty easily because I couldn't figure out where I wanted to put them and while the goalie didn't have much time to react, there was less opportunity to pull him out of position with my skating approach. I performed much better in the second half when you picked up the pucks from the blue line and they counted for twice as much as the first five.

So I was in a great spot going into the final event, which was a combination of the stick handling, passing and shooting challenges. I slowed down and focused on my passes, which made my time longer than it needed to be, but my accuracy meant that I finished before a couple of the other guys. Even though I didn't max out my points, I still had enough from the previous rounds to ensure that I finished first. I enjoyed the presentation of the giant novelty check, and got some good coverage of me at the ATM trying in vain to deposit the check in the deposit slot.

The games the following day didn't quite go our way. We won the first game and so made the final but we couldn't pull it together enough as a team and so we bowed out. The game itself was a light-hearted affair, with nobody wanting to get hurt or hurt anyone else, so checking didn't really feature. Plus we had the knowledge that it was supposed to be spectacle, so we were all guilty of maybe pushing one too many passes or trying to make the pretty play. It was good spending time with the best players in each team though. It made a huge difference when there wasn't a regular season game on the line and two points in the standings. You could actually chat with each other and enjoy the vibe.

The Brain and The Rat

I was in a press conference after scoring a hat trick in a game and the questions reminded me of the press conferences I'd seen online from previous seasons. The question I got was, "Your second goal in the first period was almost an exact copy of earlier in the season when you made the play in the defensive zone, skated hard and came into the zone as the trailer, picked up the puck from a drop pass and then fed it across the ice to the other winger in a backdoor play."

"Well, we practice particular plays and as a result, we know where we need to be and we've got good chemistry on the ice."

"Yeah but it was like a carbon copy. We've got the video overlaid and there is very little difference between the positioning."

I blinked at him. "O.. kay…?"

"And the goals on the 13th and 15th of last month were very similar as well."

"Which ones were those?"

C. G. Lambert

They told me which games they were from and I shrugged. I didn't recall every single goal and with all the games in the season, sometimes they were just a blur. If I wanted to see them, they were on nhl.com and YouTube. Don't get me wrong, the night after the game was full of snippets of memory of the plays and feelings, and what went on in the corners. But apart from the aches and bruises, by the time the next practice or the next game came around, it was as if someone had wiped a magnet over the hard drive of my brain. It was on to the next thing.

After the press conference, I was in my hotel room and I looked up the interviews that I vaguely remembered. One was someone talking about Gretzky. Apparently he would read the scores of each of the other games in the league in the papers each night and would always know which players were playing well and which were playing poorly. Over all the years that he'd been playing, he'd trained his brain to be like a database, full of trends and facts and figures, so when he was on the ice, he would know who he was up against and presumably this gave him an edge in terms of past performances. Professional athletes periodically got a bad rap for not being smart but I always thought that there was a particular skill in storing that sort of information and being able to use it.

The Forty Year Old Rookie

The other interview that I recalled was easy to find. A reporter was asking Steve Stamkos about a goal he scored on a particular date. It was admittedly only two years before but Stamkos not only knew which goal the reporter was referring to - an overtime winner - but he also knew the goalie he beat, the play leading up to it and the player who had set the screen on the goalie. Not just who'd passed him the puck or the goalie he had scored on, which was data on the game sheet and therefore available online. No, this included the guy who'd set the screen – who'd blocked the view of the goalie, so he couldn't react in time to block the shot. That didn't appear on any game sheet. None of this was from the context around the question; it was all cold recall. Stamkos at that point had scored 800 goals. I dare say that he could probably recall every single one of them. Some people train themselves so that they can memorize the digits of pi.

But me? I hadn't trained my brain in that way, so the journalist expecting me to be able to recall those goals was always going to be disappointed.

It's competitive to get into an NHL team and there are only so many slots available. If there are thirty-two teams and they dress twenty players per game, that's six hundred and forty players. They might rotate through an additional ten players from the minor league teams as a result of poor performance or injury which makes another three hundred and twenty. Round that up to a thousand. If you're the best of the best, then there may be a slot for you on the top lines. On the scoring lines if you're a forward. And if you are a goalie and you're good, then there might be a slot available there. The obvious choices.

But if you're not the world's best shot or playmaker or shot blocker, what roles are available for you? If you can fight, there might be a slot as an enforcer. This is someone who can stop the other team's players from taking liberties. If you have a lot of energy, then there might be a slot on the fourth line as a forechecker. This is someone who forces the play and gives the other guys in your team time to get their breath back. But for a cerebral type of psychotic player, there is the role of the rat.

This is someone who gets under the skin of the opposing teams' players by saying things and doing things designed to upset and unnerve, and otherwise put them off their game. Sean Avery. Brad Marchand. Steve Ott. A lot of players did such a good job of being a rat that they used that opportunity to show what else they could do. In a couple of cases, the player actually outgrew the rat role and was included because of their non-rat contributions. But they would always have that mean streak.

I had actually done a little of that as a beer leaguer. Not, you understand, in a mean way. I never talked trash or riled people up that way. No, I'd hold my stick in such a way that it would clip a player that was starting to lose their temper at something on the ice, but unrelated to me. This made their reaction so much more comical because it looked like they were just randomly lashing out. All of the things I did were innocuous, or at least never by themselves worthy of two minutes in the bin. But the reactions that they generated would usually leave us on the power play.

In the NHL, people took that to the next level and the players tended to be much more disciplined in their reactions but they weren't robots and so emotions did still boil over. Some rats would trash talk players about their relationship difficulties or their families, really personal stuff which would get your nose broken in a pub brawl if you said it out in public. Anything to get an edge on the ice. A favorite to use on rookies was to continually ask who they were and to try to see their numbers or name on the back of their jersey. The implication was that they were such nobodies that they were unrecognizable. A really nasty one was someone signing their stick and handing it to a rookie. The implication there was that they weren't even a player - just a fan.

None of those shenanigans were going to be needed because of my suit but I definitely needed to keep my head in the game. One away game, the opposing fans were incredibly loud and I told the coach I wanted to try something to help me focus. I'd wear earplugs. Not very different than professional athletes wearing headphones when they walked through the carpark of the arena on the way to the changing rooms. Listening to music helped them to focus their brain on something that wasn't going to cause stress and allow them to maximize their concentration. My theory was that it would be taken to the next level and allow me to focus on my game without any distractions on the ice. The fact was that the custom-made earplugs weren't supposed to totally block out all noise, they were just mean to diminish it. In my mind, that meant that I would still hear my teammates calling for a pass or warning me of an impending check, I would still hear the referees whistle or calls and I would definitely hear my coach calling the lines from the bench. I just wouldn't hear the cat calls and abuse from the stands and the efforts of the opposing team's rat in trying to get me off my game. That was the theory anyway.

What actually happened was very different.

The Forty Year Old Rookie

I played one home game with the earplugs and I was skating around on the ice in silence which was surreal. I didn't feed off the crowd's energy or feel as connected with the team which were both big negatives, but by the same token, I couldn't hear any of the opposing team's chirps at all. On the whole, I decided that the tradeoff wasn't worth it for the home games. My psyche would have to put up with the bad men on the other team saying mean things about me. But I did decide that I would wear them for the following away game, thinking that removing the energy of the opposing crowd might make up for the slight disconnect with the other players on my team. And not only that, I would wear them to and from the game. I had seen professional athletes from other sports getting off their buses with their headphones on, presumably with their favorite music playing but it could just as easily be some sports guru telling them in a calm voice over a background of whale song that they should breathe in for three seconds and out for three seconds.

So we got off the bus on the way into the arena, and there was a roped off section of opposition fans beside where the buses parked. When they saw us, they went ballistic, yelling at us to get back on the bus, that we were going to be beaten on the ice and that we were bums. The usual reaction to the opposing players, right? I, of course, was oblivious to all of this because I had my ear plugs in. The theory was that I could have stood next to a jet engine and only just heard a whine. Or so the sales people would have me believe.

Anyway, I only vaguely noticed the crowd and definitely didn't hear them, so I had no idea how loud they were or how nasty they were being. All I noticed was that the line of players in front of me hastened their pace a little bit. We had almost left the area when I noticed a kid out of the corner of my eye. He was maybe ten or eleven, a single person dressed in our colors standing in the middle of a crowd of opposition fans, people twice his height and three times his weight. He was holding out a poster and a sharpie, making eye contact with me. I had no idea how obnoxious those guys around him were being.

So I stopped in front of the kid, reached over for the poster and pen, and unfolded the poster. Yup, it was one of me looking particularly cheesy with a hockey stick over my shoulder, trying hard not to look like a parody of a play girl pin-up. I signed it with a flourish and returned it with a big grin. There was a lot of gesticulating and chanting from the rest of the crowd, but I was laser locked on the kid, helped no end by being able to block out the sounds, and the kid looked moved to tears. I chose to believe it was because of the importance of getting his poster of me signed

The Forty Year Old Rookie

but for all I knew, the disgusting things being said about me were truly terrible and affecting him. I figured that if he'd braved this fan section enough to get my autograph, the least I could do was give him something more to say thanks for the support, so I crouched down so I was eye to eye with him, took my team cap and put it on his head. He cried some and the adult he was with wrapped his arms around the kid and started crying too. I patted the kid on the cap and gave the adult a fist bump and then headed back to the line of players heading towards the changing rooms.

I passed a camera crew that was filming the whole thing and thought nothing of it because there are always camera crews filming. But that night in the hotel room, I got a text from one of our players with a link to the coverage that the camera crew got and it painted a truly historic picture. The noise from the fan section was incredible and they were incensed that they had to see us arrive and walk past them. You could see the unease in the other players as they passed them, giving them a wide berth. Until I walked into the frame. Apparently my normal resting face is a gormless smile and I wandered over to the kid, totally ignoring the fingers and gestures thrown my way. I was close enough for any of them to reach out and grab me but none of them did and I wasn't sure why, until I noticed that because I couldn't hear them and was only focusing on the kid, I was effectively like a lamb walking through a field of wolves. I couldn't see the danger and couldn't hear the danger, therefore there was no danger. The footage showed me signing the poster and giving the kid the hat as if I was a badass boss. I totally ignored the other team's fans and then wandered off gormlessly without a care in the world.

In the end, I stopped wearing the ear plugs because I was missing too many calls from my linemates on the ice and interestingly enough, I was actually using my hearing as an advance warning of being checked. Even with the suit, knowing when you're about to be hit was incredibly important so as to put yourself in the best position to make the next move after the check, and that was something I didn't want to give up.

Phil Collins

I was Phil Collins for fifteen years.

After dealing with the aftermath of the accident, I had to get away, so I bundled up all my belongings and moved to the other side of the country. I wasn't from a big family and in the blink of an eye, absolutely everything had been taken away from me, so there was nothing holding me to my hometown. In fact, seeing the diner where I'd go on dates with Katie, the high school where I'd attended or the library where Mom would drop me off on a Friday afternoon after school... all of those landmarks were constant reminders of what had been taken away. I was in real danger of withdrawing into myself and staying in my room and just playing video games, anything to avoid feeling. I could see it beginning to happen and so after moving, I made a concerted effort to find something, anything, to get me out of my shell. I signed up for the adult's recreational ice hockey league at the local rink and headed down for the first practice. At this point, I was chewing through what savings I had in a mid-range hotel as I tried to find work and a more permanent place to live.

I was assigned a team and after I found the right changing rooms, I settled in to get changed. Seb was the team captain of that team, and he came over and said hi as I was the new guy that season. His team list only had my first initial and surname, so naturally enough, he was convinced that I was Phil Collins rather than Peter Collins. He even introduced me to the rest of the team as Phil Collins. If you're too young to know who Phil Collins was, he was a huge songwriter, drummer and singer who wrote or co-wrote most of the songs you would have heard on the radio in the eighties. Incredibly prolific. After practice, Seb asked me where I was living and upon hearing that I was looking for somewhere to stay, he suggested I move in with him and another roommate into a three-bedroom house which was within walking distance to the rink. Naturally enough, he put my name down on the lease as Phil Collins. The rent was very reasonable and if I had roommates I figured it would force me to interact with other people, so I readily accepted.

Seb was equal parts frustrating and endearing. He was loud and obnoxious but also had a caring side as well. He said himself that he was 'the straw that stirred the drink.' If he wasn't inciting moments, then he was raising their intensity. He was a great wingman but I never quite reconciled how his party animal attitude worked with his journalism career. It wasn't until I had known him for a while that I realized that the journalism thing was really an excuse to get into events and that he half-arsed the whole article writing thing afterwards. He was forever getting suspended or put on performance plans and then redeeming himself with some insightful exposé that he wrote down verbatim from someone he met at a party or a friend of a friend who knew some juicy piece of gossip. He must have done research and corroboration because the stories always stood up to the inevitable scrutiny. But he was a magnetic personality and people opened up to him, so maybe journalism wasn't such a bad fit for him after all.

As for me, I never really developed a career per se, more a succession of coding jobs which ended either in getting laid off or fired as the role was offshored or dissolved, or restructured into something involving AI. Every couple of years, I would wonder if I should retrain into Data Science but after the third time of being laid off because some senior manager had decided that AI could do my job, becoming one of the AI folks seemed like a pig becoming a butcher. Like joining the enemy.

C. G. Lambert

Andrew wasn't the original third roommate. We actually had a mechanic who worked at a garage nearby. Her name was Meredith and she was covered in tattoos. I saw her in a bikini once briefly and I didn't know where to look. They were quite stunning artistically but looking closely at them would have been a bit leery, so I avoided doing so too closely. Seb on the other hand was not similarly restrained. "Nice tatts," was misheard as "Nice tits," which led to one of the heated conversations that both of them seemed to enjoy. She called him a pig and he professed his innocence and I sat there embarrassed with an angel on one shoulder saying, "I don't like it when Mommy and Daddy fight," and the devil on the other shoulder saying, "Just fuck already."

After Meredith left Larry, another of the guys from the ice hockey team moved in but he didn't pay his ice time and then he didn't pay his share of the bills. Soon we had to kick him out because he wasn't paying his share of the rent either. Funnily enough, we had the local police attending one of our games because he was wanted for writing bad checks but had moved out of the house by then. The police presence almost doubled the attendance for that particular game.

The third room was left vacant for a while after that. Periodically, Seb would put it back on various websites trying to find someone else, and he had a lot of interest because the rent was cheap but the location wasn't the best for those wanting to work because it was in a bit of a black hole when it came to public transport, so even with the cheap rent, we couldn't find many people who were interested.

That was until Andrew came along. He worked not far off at one of the Big Pharma research labs nearby. We never quite figured out exactly what he did for work but it was definitely something to do with research and development involving materials. Perfect when it came to developing the suit. He would periodically have work colleagues around to the house for a beer or something stronger but they were always weird situations. I sometimes thought that he was selling the results of his research on the side because none of these "work colleagues" ever came back and there were frequently raised voices or arguments coming from his bedroom. There was also a general suss vibe from the people he did bring back.

But he paid the rent and bills on time and did his share of the chores, so as good of a roommate as you could expect.

I'm not sure how successful I was with resisting being a total shut in. Sure, I had my ice hockey but as the jobs ticked by, I found it easier to find remote work rather than having to go into the office. On the face of it, this was a good situation to be in because of the house being in a black hole when it came to public transport but in terms of being around other actual human beings, it didn't really help. But over time, the grief... well you never really get over something like that. But over time, the grief wasn't as debilitating and I could live with it.

The beard started off as just not shaving between contracts but then it sort of stayed and I liked it. I would joke that it kept me warm when I was on the bench but truth be told, it made me look pretty badass and definitely very beer league.

In a lot of ways, my career in professional ice hockey was another situation where I cut off all connections to my old world in favor of the new. Originally, I turned my back on the life I had with Mom and Dad and Katie and the Bump to escape the grief. And then I turned my back on Seb and Andrew in favor of the possibilities that the suit brought with it. When I was giving myself a hard time, I would wonder if there was something callous about me given how I was able to move on so quickly from losing Seb and Andrew. And in my darkest times, I wondered if my heart was calloused and if I would ever be able to love again.

Sally's

Most of our games started at seven in the evening, local time. However, there were a bunch of matinees during the season where, by the time you'd played the game and showered and dealt with the press, you'd find yourself with post-game energy on a Monday at six or seven in the evening, but with nothing to do and a practice the next morning. In the NHL of yesteryear, that might have led to an all-night drinking session and a guilty practice the following morning but in the more professional age, that would be frowned upon. I was still taking public transport, so by the time I got off the bus near my apartment, it was still early.

There was a sports bar near the apartment so I popped my head in on the way past. It was roomy and clean, and there were TV screens everywhere showing various games from various leagues across most of the available sports. This early on a Monday, it was also devoid of customers. I wandered over to the bartender, a hipster chick with a septum, a mini-beanie and an attitude.

"Hi, what can I get you?"

"Uh... hi... Sally. What time do you close?"

"We're open till one."

"On a Monday night?"

She looked guilty. "Well, if it's still dead at ten, we usually call it quits."

"Nice one. I'll be finished way before then. Could I get the replay of the NHL game on that screen? Then can I get a half and half - lemonade and lager, and maybe a plate of wings? If you see me finish the drink, can you bring a carafe of water over and keep it topped up?"

Sally smiled and nodded. "Do you want to set up a tab?"

I shrugged and pulled out my per diem. "Nah, I'll settle up now if that's OK?"

"Sure, that's eight for the beer and fifteen for the wings so twenty-three."

I gave her a fifty, told her to keep the change and headed over to my seat. The screen quickly flicked over to the replay of the game I had just played. Now that was a new perspective. Watching the game as a consumer instead of a professional wasn't like having a session with the video coach where they went frame by frame and asked you what you were thinking on every error. This was the version where the drama of the contest was much more important than the possible improvements you might make. Or the justification for passing right instead of left.

Sally flicked the audio of the bar to the feed from the game and brought my drink over. I smiled my thanks and then returned to reliving the game from my seat. I didn't realize the effect until Sally brought out the wings. She looked at me sideways as she dropped them off.

"Are you okay?" she asked.

I looked at her confused.

"You're twitching and bobbing and weaving all over the place," she said as she left.

"I guess I'm a little too involved in the game," I explained as she returned to the bar. And that was exactly it. I didn't know if it was muscle memory or just recognizing the game situations and thinking about what I would do in each one but I was doing the beginning of the motions for what my brain was telling my body it should do. Weirdly enough, it was only my upper body doing the movements.

But watching the game seemed to have a soothing effect on my brain, and by the time the coverage had finished and I had followed up my shandy and wings with about three carafes of water, I felt like I had decompressed. I certainly didn't think I had a full set of notes on my performance like the video coach would be going through the next day but my brain's requirement to revisit every critical situation in the game had been alleviated slightly.

I went to Sally's bar after each of the midweek matinee games. There weren't a whole bunch of them but I guess the regularity of them made my presence predictable. The second time, the cook came out from the kitchen and watched the game from the table beside mine, occasionally glancing between me and the TV screen, and only scuttling back into the kitchen when another customer ordered some food.

I was surprised that they stayed open on Monday and Tuesday nights as I was frequently the only person in the bar. But one night I walked in and there was someone already sitting at my table. No problem, there were plenty of other seats around. The best view of the largest TV screen was achieved from any of four seats in the middle of the floor, so I sat myself down at the table beside my usual one instead.

The person at my normal seat was a young lady, made up for a night on the town. She was nursing a tall glass with a wedge of lemon in it but was laser focused on the door as if she was trying to manifest the presence of someone just by looking at it.

Sally dropped my drink off with a smirk. I couldn't figure out what she was tickled by - I wasn't so precious that I expected my table to be My Table. With me wanting to watch the game and the young lady watching the door, we were facing each other on different tables. I couldn't help but strike up a conversation.

"Are you waiting for someone?"

She glanced up and assessed me in a split second. Her eyes widened slightly as she took in the stitches on my chin and the bruising on my cheek. She flashed a smile which disappeared as soon as it hit her lips. "I heard a pro hockey player comes here after his games, so I'm going to get him to buy me a drink," she said, flicking her eyes back to the door.

I smiled. "Oh wow, that's great! Do you know who it is?" Behind her on the screen, they were going through the lineups for the game, and it was still disconcerting seeing my face so large on a TV screen.

She shook her head slightly. "No, I heard it from my sister who heard it from her doorman who heard it from someone who works here. But you have to stop talking to me when he arrives. I don't want him to think that we're together." She laughed as if that was ludicrous and then turned it into a cough when she realized that might be a rude thing to say.

"No, of course. But how will you know it's him?"

She shrugged. "He'll look like a professional athlete of course. He'll be tall and muscly."

Behind her, the first period had just started. "Oh? I heard that professional hockey players couldn't be too muscly because it got in the way of their flexibility…"

She looked very much like she was ignoring me. "…and most of them look like they're tall because they're on ice skates which add two or three inches to their height."

She stopped staring at the door to the bar for long enough to assess me for a little longer. "And what do you do for a living? Construction?"

"What makes you say that?"

"It looks like you've been in a fight."

I felt the stitches and smiled. "Yeah, it does look like that, doesn't it?"

"So you're not going to tell me?"

"Maybe later. So what happens when this pro player walks in?"

She looked concerned. "You will stop talking to me then, won't you?"

I held up my hands. "Of course. Far be it for me to stand in the way of true love."

She looked satisfied at my response. Behind her on the big screen, I had scored my first goal of the afternoon and was celebrating with the team. While the puck was retrieved, the coverage flicked to some charts of my scoring progression and how I was performing relative to other players in history. Sally brought over my wings with a full smile. She could see the scenario playing out.

"Hey Sally. Did you know a pro hockey player was coming here to your bar tonight?"

She played along, her eyes widening. "No, I didn't know that. Who is it?"

I turned to my new friend. "I'm not sure. Apparently we'll know when they walk in."

Sally shrugged as she walked past. "Meh, I don't care about hockey players. Now football players, that's more my style."

I smiled wryly at Sally as she headed back to the bar. Touché, Madame!

For the next twenty minutes, I watched the game and the young lady watched the front door and she never gave me her name and I never asked. We'd chat briefly before her focus would go back to the front door as if she was afraid she'd miss someone coming into the bar unless she was alert at all times.

"So what do you do for a living?" I asked as behind her I scored the third of my goals.

"I'm a secretary in an office. It's a temp job."

"Ah that's cool - you're the face of the company, right?"

She looked at me as if I had two heads.

"Not really. I hate it but I need the money. People are jerks."

I blinked. "People are jerks?"

She rolled her eyes. "There's a constant stream of people. Wanting something. Couriers. People coming in for job interviews. People from out of town. People sending things. Find the mailroom and leave me alone. For fuck's sake."

"Yeah, that can be tough."

Behind her, it was coming to the part of the game where I took a hard hit into the boards and the suit didn't do enough to protect me - it probably stopped me from getting a concussion but it didn't stop my face from going into the glass and getting the cut and bruise on my face. I got up to leave the bar, knowing that the surprised look on my face as I went into the glass had been captured by the cameras and they would be replaying the impact over and over again because it looked funny.

"Hey. Nice chatting with you, best of luck with that hockey player." She looked up and smiled a little sadly at me. "You were asking about my stitches?" She nodded, obviously readying herself for a story or maybe just a throwaway line like 'You should have seen the other guy.' Instead, I pointed to the TV behind her and then headed for the door, waving to Sally and the cook. "Later Sally. See you, Raphael!" I was dying to see the look on her face as she realized who I was but it would have ruined the effect.

Sally's bar was as close to a local as I had for the season and I only turned up after a weekday matinee so there weren't that many middle of the day games, but whenever I did the number of other customers would grow. It was a weird experience in the first place, watching a game for the enjoyment of the game as opposed to for a learning experience. But then watching the game with a bunch of fans was even weirder. Nobody was pissed or drunk because it was so early in the evening. And the only thing I'd heard of which came close to the vibe was one of those cinema shows where people would yell at the screen - your Rocky Horror Picture Show or even The Sound of Music. There would be bits in those movies where you would yell something at the screen and you were contributing to the evening. In my case, early on when there were maybe six or seven other people there, there would be a groan when I would be taken into the boards. Or a quiet clap when I scored. By the time we were getting close to the end of the season, the place would have twenty or thirty fans in there, all with their jerseys on and cheering every goal or hit and booing the penalty calls which went against the team. By this time, Raphael would stay in the kitchen and Sally had two other waitresses helping her out.

Periodically, she'd come up to me and tell me that one of the patrons had wanted to buy me a drink and that she'd told them that I only ever had water, and then I would go over and have a chat with them. I'd say something generic and forgettable but always end up thanking them for their support and telling them to tip the staff well. Occasionally I'd sign something for them like a napkin or a menu. I never wanted to be followed home so when it was time to leave and usually before the game coverage finished, I'd head into the kitchen and say goodnight to everybody and then head out the back door into the alleyway behind the bar. It connected two streets, so even if someone was watching the front door, they wouldn't see me leave. Eventually, Sally got a photo of me sitting on my stool with the bar full behind me and had it framed and put on the wall.

Sleeping Beauty

When you're in the meat and potatoes of the season, the systems and processes put in place mean the players can focus on their game. Nobody has to think about what they're doing and it all comes off like clockwork. There are usually a ton of moving parts and the professionals behind the scenes work hard so the players can perform on the ice. Sometimes the fates align and the backup plan to the backup plan has to come into play.

We were past the trade deadline and had already clinched a playoff spot. The Presidents' Trophy was a possibility and we were over the hump and looking to make it to the playoffs healthy and firing on all cylinders. We had the first leg of a home-and-home with one of our divisional rivals. The plan was to play our home game, fly to their city straight afterwards, arrive at the hotel in the early hours and then get into the usual game day routine. Head to the rink in the morning, have a skate, and go back to the hotel; then team meal, nap in the afternoon and then back to the rink; warm-ups and then the game.

But the first thing that stopped that was the blizzard which came out of nowhere and stopped all air traffic in the area. That went all night and it wasn't apparent until halfway through our home game. The backup plan was to head to an airport hotel, stay overnight and get the plane in the morning when the weather cleared.

In the morning, we headed onto the tarmac ready to go. The equipment guys had already loaded the gear into the cargo hold. Then the captain came on the intercom. "Uh… this is your captain speaking. We're being held up because of a slight technical hitch and we're just waiting on a replacement part for the engine. We've been told that it's en route and that we should be underway in half an hour. Apologies for the delay."

Even though I had earned my spot on the team and was old enough to pass for a veteran, I still had a seat with the rookies and fringe players, up the front of the plane just behind the coaches and managers. This included the travel manager and she was working the phone hard in the seat two rows in front of me. I heard her talking to bus drivers and hiring flight people for the next thirty minutes as she put in place contingency plans left and right.

They were definitely needed when it turned out that the wrong part had been delivered and that the plane was not going to be operational until the next day. Cue groans from both players and staff as plan C was wheeled out. We would be taking a charter plane instead. The charter company operated from the same airport where we found ourselves and they would be sending their plane over to pick us and our gear up.

The plane pulled up alongside ours and the equipment guys deplaned, heading to the cargo doors to transfer the gear. The players and management trooped over and boarded the new plane, ready to continue playing cards or watching a show on their tablet, or in the case of a couple of the guys, actually reading something. I figured it would be helpful to get the gear transferred as soon as possible so instead of heading across the tarmac to the new plane, I strolled over to the cargo doors. "You guys need a hand?"

The equipment manager smiled lopsidedly. "No, that's fine thanks, we've got it." I don't know if you've ever seen the amount of gear that a hockey team carts from game to game but you might know the standard hockey bag that players tow behind them on the way to practices and games. Its long, usually fabric, has wheels at one end and a telescopic handle on the other. Anyway, imagine you had one of those for each of the twenty players, plus spare gear, plus sticks - not just the typical two per player, we're talking six to ten. Plus skate sharpening gear. We're talking about a sizable chunk of stuff. I ignored the equipment manager and joined the conveyor belt of humans connecting the cargo hold of one plane to that of the other and hoisted gear bags along with the equipment guys.

We got everything squared away and then rejoined the team on the charter plane, just in time to see the lights in the cabin flicker and then go out. Five minutes later, the new captain came onto the intercom. A different problem but the same situation. We would be delayed. The equipment manager made eye contact with me and rolled his eyes. Potentially a waste of a lot of effort. The travel manager was calmly talking on the phone, obviously working on Plan D. Another half hour went by as there were discussions about whether the issue was serious or not and then the decision was made that we would bus to the other city. By this time, it was late morning and even with the travel time and stopping on the way for lunch, we could make it to the hotel in time to check in and have a nap. So we were nowhere even close to being in danger of missing the game. It was just about how much of our routine would end up being disrupted.

The bus pulled up and the guys got on board. I stayed behind to help the equipment guys again. Then, just when we'd finished loading up, the bus pulled out and drove off. I glanced around. The equipment manager looked worried and pulled out his cellphone to call the coach and let him know our team was now shorthanded by one star player, and that they should turn the bus around. But to no avail. There was definitely cell reception on the tarmac but we tried everyone and we couldn't get through. In a city this large, it seemed inconceivable that a bus wouldn't have reception but there it was.

"They'll get reception soon but it will be a ball ache turning around and coming back for you, so why don't you come with us?"

"Yeah, sure, that's no problem. Why did they leave without you guys?"

"The bus is too small. It can only fit the coaches and players."

"Oh, okay. How will you guys get there?"

"We'll get a hire car and head up. We'll go straight to the arena though, to load in."

"Where will the bus go?"

"The bus will drop the team off at the hotel and then go to the arena for us to unload. It will then go back to the hotel to pick up the players and bring them back to the arena. You can come with us to the arena and then catch up with them at the hotel or just wait at the arena. Up to you."

I shrugged. "Less hassle to just go straight to the arena, I guess. I can't get lost or miss the game if I'm there. As long as we tell them where I am once we get back in touch with them, that should be fine."

So you'd imagine that's where the adventure stopped, right? We were operating on the contingency of a backup plan of a 'what if'. That's where things would have stopped if we were just relying on the fates. But then humans being what we are, things went a little further awry.

We got in touch with the bus when they were half an hour down the road, and let them know that I was fine, thanks, and that I would meet them at the arena. The equipment manager located the hire car desks and one actually had a car available. He grinned when we walked over to where it was parked. "I, uh, had to upgrade due to your height. We can't have one of our players sitting in a car with insufficient leg room." I grinned back when I saw what he meant. It was a luxury car that could fit the four of us with ample space. We were over an hour behind them but that would easily be made up by the bus having to get to the hotel through the inner-city traffic, so it would be perfect timing for the equipment guys in the arena.

We stopped off on the way for lunch and I had my standard pre-game meal of a plate of spaghetti and meatballs. The others had burgers or fajitas with fries.

On the way, when we were stopped in traffic, the manager turned to me. "Uh... hey it's been great hanging out with you but when we get to the rink, we can't have you helping with the equipment. I mean we appreciate it and all, but there's insurance that means we're not covered if something happens, and we're a union house so we can't have anyone outside the union doing anything related to equipment. As I say, we really appreciate it, but..."

I blinked. "Oh! Yeah of course, sorry, I didn't realize I was making things awkward for you guys. Sure, sure. That's fine."

"It's nice to know that you're willing to roll up your sleeves. Appreciate it."

When we arrived, the equipment manager showed the security guard his pass and we were waved into the bowels of the arena. They parked up and we met the bus. The equipment guys politely pointed me to the visitors' changing rooms and so I went and hung out there. They came in soon enough, laying out the gear and getting everything just so, with the jerseys on the hangers and name plates over every stall. Our standard routine dictated that we'd have a pre-game nap, so I found the only room with a bed - the medical bay - and crawled onto the bed and lay down. Within minutes, I was asleep.

As soon as my eyes opened, I knew something was wrong.

I reached for my phone and tried to turn it on so I could see in the dark but there was no juice. Trying to phone so many people from the airport and on the way from there to here had drained the battery. I winced. I hadn't fully charged it last night either, so it wasn't like it had started on full charge. Outside, I could hear crowd noise. How long had I slept for?!

I got off the bed and fumbled on the wall for the light switch. Eventually I found it and got ready to sprint the short distance to the changing room to get ready for the game. They surely hadn't started already, had they?!

But the door was locked. And instead of a button in the doorknob to open the door on this side, there was another keyhole. I wouldn't be able to open it myself. I screamed and yelled and pummeled on the door with my fists. But of course, my super suit with the strength to possibly break through the door was in the changing room.

After a maddening length of time, someone eventually opened the door and I practically bowled them over in the mad rush to get to the changing room.

Now, let's pause to examine some of the weirder rules of some beer hockey leagues that I had played in. One league stated that if a player didn't get on the ice in the first period, then they couldn't play for the rest of the game. They had to have a minimum level of gear on, so one shin pad, one elbow pad and one glove on, plus skates of course. They had to be on the ice before the buzzer at the end of the period. As I lived so close to the rink, occasionally I was the last one to the game and therefore a little late onto the ice. I wasn't the only one. With the stakes being lower in the beer league, we often even started a game without a goalie as they weren't quite fully dressed in time for the opening faceoff.

Now I got dressed in a mad rush and did that weird sprint that you only ever do while wearing skates and stepping on the black rubber flooring that does not chip your skate blades. As I made it to the benches, I could see that the game had indeed already started, that we were halfway through the first period, and that we were 5-2 down already.

I didn't make eye contact with anyone on the bench but jumped over the boards for the first player changing and started skating hard. I was thinking in phases. Phase one had been getting changed as quickly as I could. Achieved. Phase two was getting on the ice in the first period. Achieved. Phase three was playing so well that everyone would forgive me for missing the first ten minutes of an NHL game. So I was like a man possessed. I skated hard and kept my momentum going by staying on my edges and not gliding much at all. In my first shift, I dug the puck out of a scrum along the boards, hit an open man with a sharp pass and joined the rush, picking up a juicy rebound and tucking it home for a goal. Not a goal scorer's goal but some way towards restitution for my delayed start. And it was such a relief when I made it back to the benches.

"Nice of you to join us, Peter," Coach said, his face trying to show anger as well as thankfulness at the same time, making him look insane. He had his hands full though, undoing the changes in the lines that he had been forced to put together with my absence, and going back to some form of normal. I was super focused on what was happening on the ice, in part to avoid any angry stares from the coaching staff boring holes into the back of my head but mostly to catch up on the game and who was playing well and who wasn't.

And I was on fire. I picked up the game in the palm of my hands and dictated what happened on the ice while I was on it. With one exception. My passes ripped along the ice and went straight onto our player's sticks. My shots found their way onto the net more often than not and seemed to be destined for one or another of the four corners of the goal. My speed never dropped below a solid sprint and I was dodging checks and laying the body with great intensity. But I couldn't win a face-off to save my life. I wised up after five or six losses in a row and started calling my wingers in to take the face-offs instead of me. I wasn't just losing against their top center but against them all. Better to tag out and give someone else a chance than forcing myself to lose over and over again. Quite frequently when our winger lost the draw, I was able to swoop in on the puck before their other players could capitalize on winning and we would come away with the puck anyway.

By the end of the first period, we were down 5-3. By the end of the second, we were leading by a single goal. By the end of the game, we had scored eight unanswered goals and I was sitting on an eight-point night. I came off the ice and slumped in my stall, exhausted, happy and speechless. My teammates were ecstatic with the come from behind victory and there was much shouting and slapping of shoulders in the room. Coach came in and said a few words of congratulations and made eye contact with me. I knew there would be questions asked and answers expected but not here and not now. I was grinning widely as I celebrated with the team. My smile froze on my face when I looked down and saw my special hockey suit tucked under my seat, still on its hanger and unworn.

I couldn't dwell on that and what it might mean because the press came in and had a lot of questions for me. Starting with the obvious.

"Peter, where were you for the start of the game?"

"Look, there was a logistical error made and I will address that with Coach. If there's a punishment involved, I'll take it. We can certainly talk about the game though."

They were not happy with getting a non-answer. The disappearing star was only just eclipsed by a phenomenal points effort. "An 8-point game doesn't come along very often, a very special game for you no doubt. But how many might you have gotten with a full sixty minutes on the ice?"

"Well, you know as well as I do that the only person on the ice for the full sixty minutes is the goalie but I know what you're saying."

The rest of the press interactions were equally as unsatisfying for them and eventually the questions petered out and I was able to get changed and head towards the bus for the trip back to the hotel.

Coach was waiting for me before I got on the bus and pulled me to one side.

"Okay, what happened?"

"I fell asleep in the medical bay." Coach just looked at me. "It took me a while to get out." I could tell that it was hard to believe. Which made it believable. Why would anyone come up with such a bullshit excuse unless it was true? "Look, I'm telling the truth. There's nothing seedy or weird. I came straight to the arena. I had a pregame nap. I don't know if someone saw me in there or what, but it took a little while to find someone from the arena to let me out. It's my bad, though. So obviously any punishment coming my way, I accept."

Coach laughed. "If you can produce an eight-point night on command and all it needs is to be locked in the medibay for your nap, I think we can arrange that! No problems, we'll make an announcement that no further punishment will be forthcoming. An innocent mistake was made. Now get back on the bus, we're heading back to the hotel."

On the bus, there was a raucous response - lots of bawdy innuendo and a hell of a lot of speculation. "Were they twins? I bet they were twins! Is the coach going to bench you?"

I laughed along with the boys and played the bashful 'aw shucks' but I just wanted to be alone to think. Some of the others went out afterwards for a drink but I told them all that I was bushed and headed for reception to check in and get my room key.

As soon as I was alone, I shook my head as I replayed discovering my suit in my stall over and over again. If I hadn't been wearing it, then…?

The Date

The restaurant was high-end, the lights low, and the music subdued. They didn't have a multi-month long wait list but everyone was dressed nicely and there was the smell of money in the air. She was stunning in a long shimmer of silk, her hair done up very nicely and wearing subtle jewelry. We had just ordered when she leaned back, taking a sip of her gin and tonic and asked me how my life differed now from what it had been before I was signed as a professional athlete.

"I guess my life before was probably very much what yours is like now. I was on a five day on, two off cycle. Each workday feels the same, nine to five. You have your travel time and your breaks, you have your water cooler and your office hours, and it's pretty predictable. Periodically, you have to go somewhere for an offsite or a meeting but those exceptions just prove the cubicle law."

She smiled. "I'm aware," she said.

"Even if you have Working From Home, it's the same. You have work that needs doing and you have your meetings, and you sit in front of your computer and do your thing."

"And now?"

Now it was my turn to smile. "Forget your five on and two off. You don't have that regular rhythm, which means that you can't do cooking lessons or go to night school and get a degree or anything that requires a day of the week commitment. You have a game and that game is either at home or away. If it's an away game, you have to travel before and afterwards. If it's at home, you might have practice the next day or travel for the next game. If you're in the East, you might have a couple of hours drive to the game if it's against your nearest rival but if you're playing against someone in the opposite conference, you might have a six-hour flight and an hour in a bus to and from the airport. You might have a road trip of a week or two of away games with nothing but hotels and planes between each game. You might get a day off on that trip to have a look around and you might get a day off if there's a long layover between home games."

"So I imagine game days are pretty regimented."

"Absolutely. The more clockwork they can make things, the fewer things that can go wrong. The fewer choices you have to make, the less energy you waste considering new information."

"And when you're on a road trip, you're either flying or playing."

"Yup. A bit of a waste, right? Going to thirty other cities and not really seeing much of them. Just the airport, hotel and arena."

She smiled sadly. "A bit like when I was working out of a suitcase doing audit work. All you ever saw was an office, a hotel, a taxi and the airport. You could have been anywhere and everything was interchangeable. It made me really appreciate my time off."

"But the difference is when you have a few home games together in a row. You might have a practice day but that's over after a few hours, and the rest of the time is yours. Then you might have a day off. You have to have time to rest after all. Your body needs some down time. We've got a couple of those during this season. A home game and then another one four days later. They have two practices in the time between but that still gives you a full day off plus two practice days."

She looked at me over the edge of her glass, a sparkle in her eye. "And what do you get up to on those days off? Or even on the practice days after you've showered and headed home?"

I smiled back ruefully. "Some of the guys don't do too well. Especially the younger guys. They go gambling or partying. Some do drugs. A lot of them drink. They're athletes, so they're in great condition, and professional athletes so they have money, and depending on the city they play in, they could be quite famous. That breeds certain behaviors. And you can only do so much to counter that, especially if someone gets led astray."

"And you?"

I was surprised. Was she suggesting I was a party animal? "To tell the truth, I was never a party animal. Adding money and fame to the equation just makes you more of who you are, and I am perhaps the most boring person you'll ever meet."

She blinked in surprise. I guess most dates concentrated on talking themselves up, rather than the opposite. "So this routine repeats all the way through the season?"

"Oh, no! It kind of goes from October to May but they give you a couple of days off over Christmas and then there's the All-Star Game Break. Sometimes, when a star player gets selected for the All-Star Game, they decide to take a rest instead of attending the game because their body needs it. The League loves it when they do that!"

"Then in May?"

"Ah, then there are the playoffs. That's when everything changes. You do less travel because you're locked in a series with one other team. But there's so much pressure and focus on the game that you don't get any time off. Some teams even book out hotels for their home games so then all of the players can be together with no distractions of family or girlfriends or anything external. Say goodbye to Daddy, kids, he's off to the playoffs."

"Wow, that's terrible."

"Is it? For a chance to win the Stanley Cup? We're professional athletes. We get to play a game for big bucks and the whole thing is about that end of the season and getting over the line. If you're not ready to make that sacrifice, there are hundreds of players who are willing."

"What about romance? When do you make time for that?" That sparkle in her eye again.

I smiled back and took a sip of my water. "Well, you can always find time for the right person. Tell me more about you. Are you still in audit?"

Something in her demeanor told me that wasn't an area she wanted to talk about. "I did my time and got my qualification, and then I started seeing one of the partners."

I frowned in quizzical puzzlement. "Aren't most partners a little older?"

She looked bemused. "He was on the right side of fifty and I was in my early twenties."

"Oh, wow. Was he a partner in your department?"

Her smirk looked positively devilish. "Yes. Technically he wasn't my boss. He was my boss's boss's boss. We actually got married, believe it or not. On the beach, a destination wedding. It was glorious."

I paused and then respectfully continued. "So... do you mind me asking what happened? I mean, I assume you broke up? He's not at home waiting for you, is he?" I laughed a little to let her know I wasn't serious but the thought of a sixty-year-old guy waiting for her while she was out on a date was a little heartbreaking.

"Oh, no. We broke up after a year. The thing about partners at any of the finance or accountancy or legal firms is that they spend all of their time in the office. That's a great place to meet them but after you're married, that's where they'll spend all their time. Regardless of what they tell you beforehand, it's a lifestyle."

"Oh, I'm sorry to hear that. That's a pity. And so, what do you do now?"

"Now? Well, I'm still getting alimony because I haven't found anyone I want to marry who will give me more than my allowance. So that makes it hard to meet the right guy because I'm always comparing them with him. Do you know what I mean?"

"You mean their ethics, sense of humor and personality?"

"No, how much they make and whether they'll want a prenup. I can't put my 'now' at risk for a 'maybe' future. That's just not smart."

"Yeah, I can see that." I made polite conversation for the rest of the evening but made my excuses to avoid the offer of coffee back at her place. She was probably telling her friends about the clueless guy who didn't understand what that offer meant but in my case, I really wanted nothing to do with her.

I was actually glad that she was so obviously attracted by the promise of my upcoming wealth. That made it easy to see her and easy again to steer clear of her. What worried me was someone that I'd wake up to after three or five years who decided that it was the right time to jump ship, taking half of my (admittedly ill-gotten) gains with her.

C. G. Lambert

I was touched that so many people approached me with offers of a date with their cousin or their friend, or usually, their friend's mother. I guessed that if the most famous hockey player in the world was dating their friend or their cousin or their aunt, then all of a sudden, their social standing would improve. Plus, they'd have some pretty serious bragging rights. Who knows, maybe I would pay for the whole family to fly to the mountains or the beach? Pretty high potential reward for only a little risk, right?

It was a pretty obvious fact that any single heterosexual man of a certain level of wealth would find himself in need of a wife. And a lot of people were very interested in being that matchmaker. One media event that the team lent players to was a charity fashion show. To see the hockey players in suits walking down the catwalk and practicing their steely model looks. The media loved it because the players were lauded if they could pull it off or sneered at if they couldn't. The players loved it because they got to be in the changing area backstage with all of the pretty female models and the models got to hang out with the players after the show. Win, win, win, right?

It was hilarious because when the single players (I imagine the veteran's wives weren't interested in letting their husbands participate) were getting phone numbers after the show and were

The Forty Year Old Rookie

ready to hit the best nightclubs afterwards, one of the players came jogging over to me and gave me a piece of paper. I looked between him and the paper, not really understanding. "What's this?"

"It's a phone number."

"Did one of the models give it to you to give to me?" I asked. Convinced that I was being punked.

"Oh yeah, absolutely. We're going to go out now but she demanded that I give you the number."

"Which one gave you the number?"

"The skinny blonde one on the end."

I looked at him in disbelief. "They're all skinny blondes, man. Could you be a little more specific?"

He grinned at me. "The one on the left." She was painfully thin but gorgeous in a very obvious way.

I caught her eye and waved. She made a phone gesture and mouthed 'Call me.' Well, I thought it was 'call me' but the last word wasn't 'me.'

"Yeah, that's her. She said that she told her mother that you'll ring her and she's expecting your call. Have a good night, man. See you at practice."

Booze

Beer league is beer league because of the beer. It shows that the experience is more about camaraderie and a relaxed level of competition, as well as that, the skill level is on the lower side. But what it also shows is hockey's long association with drinking beer. Looking back on my experiences, it should have come as no surprise how many of the notable episodes revolved around drinking. Even if going out for a drink was merely the pretense for team building or developing the relationships within the team. And you can guarantee that professional athletes with low body fat percentages, salaries ten to twenty times the average and very little in the way of responsibilities would find themselves in some novel situations.

We had put together an impressive stretch of wins and we had a series of home games, meaning that we weren't out on the road, so the coaches gave us a full day off. One thing led to another and before you could say 'tenuous reason to celebrate', we found ourselves heading out to a bar for a drinking session.

Every team has a social committee, whether they're official or formed by those with connections to the social scene of the city. Plugging into the social fabric was essential to accommodate a group of twenty or so descending onto a watering hole. Phones around the city were pinging with the location and meeting time that would kick off the evening, and taxis converged on the Rolling K bar downtown. We had a section roped off protected by a bouncer and, although it was early, the private sanctum had been infiltrated by a selection of the local beauties.

We had our own side of the long horseshoe shaped bar which formed one wall of our private section. Someone had foolishly put their card on the bar to start a tab and it was getting a good work out. I was pacing myself, as I'd given up serious drinking sometime after university and I didn't have the years of practice metabolizing alcohol as my teammates had.

Things were going well, with four or five of the guys holding court with the same number of young ladies and the rest of us spinning off-color jokes or talking shit when I had to head off to the restroom. I made sure to nod to the bouncer in the hope that he would recognize me on my return. I could imagine the raucous ribbing I would get if he did not let me past the velvet rope. It would all be good natured of course but I would feel pretty bad if the biggest memories of me at the end of the year were all the places that had barred me because they couldn't believe that I was a player on the team. Not good for the psyche.

On the way back from the restroom, I was steeling myself for the big test when I felt a hand on my arm and looked down into a pair of the most piercing sapphire blue eyes I had ever seen. "Are you guys in a band?"

She would have been maybe twenty, accompanied by three friends, all dolled up with one eye on 'classy' and the other on advertising all they had to offer. The overall effect on me was a desire to put a blanket over their shoulders. The music was loud, which meant I had to lean down and get my ear near her mouth, which I used as an excuse to keep as much of her cleavage out of my eyeline as possible.

"We're hockey players," I told her at high volume.

She nodded as if that was obvious. "And are you their coach?"

I gave her a wry smile. "No, I'm a player too."

Her face didn't quite say 'Sure you are, grandpa,' but I figured she had learned how not to let her face instantly display what her mind was thinking.

"Do you want to meet the guys?" I asked, more to get me back to the party rather than in an altruistic move.

Their little faces lit up. I led them back to the private area and past the bouncer (result!). When the boys saw who I was leading back to them, a huge cheer went up and all of a sudden I was flavor of the month with bawdy jokes and the repeated suggestion that I still had game and there was life in the old dog yet. I good-naturedly accepted their compliments and headed back to the bar to replenish my drink and symbolically relinquish any claim I might be seen to have on any of our new companions. The last thing I needed was a reputation as a ladies' man when the ladies were only just out of high school. Don't get me wrong, that would actually be a badge of honor amongst the guys. But I couldn't think of a single thing I had in common with them. What do you talk about? So... where are you investing your 401k? I was no good the first time around and now it was twenty years later. I had no memory of the non-existent skill of seduction and no intention of using that skill on someone who was old enough to be my daughter.

By and large, the guys were respectful around women and even when under the influence, there were no shenanigans or incidents to bring the team or league into disrepute. I'd love to say that I was one of the calm older heads who kept an eye on the guys and made sure everybody got home okay, and that heated situations were diffused skillfully but truth be told, I waited until the guys with families left and then made my excuses also. That ensured that I didn't get a reputation as someone who flaked and I still got to enjoy some of the evening without having a splitting headache the following day. And as I'd gotten older, the intensity of my hangovers had increased, so I wasn't tortured the following morning with the ramifications of my actions. I guess I could have played the star player card - there seemed to be enough deference to where I stood in the pecking order that I could have just not turned up because of who I was but that was no way to bond as a team. Besides, the guys were a great bunch of fellas.

We did have an incident where I was able to show a little bit of leadership. While women were making inroads into roles in professional hockey, it was still pretty much a boy's club. There were some clubs with women assistant coaches and some with physios but there weren't many. We had a female physio, Sasha. Small hands but when she got her elbows involved, there wasn't a knotted muscle she couldn't loosen. Anyway, I was talking to one of our rookies, Mikhail, who had just been called up early in the season and he was a little on the cocky side. Big ego. I was chatting with him, trying to see if he realized that his call up might have been the coaches trying him out in the bigs for eight or nine games before sending him back down to minors. If he played fewer than ten games in the big team, then his three-year entry-level contract would slide and that season wouldn't count towards the three years covered by the contract. So it was a great way for the coaching staff to see how his development was going but a bit of a tease too, because it extended the time you were on your lowest paying contract in your career. I was being gentle about it because I didn't know if he knew about the slide and by the way he was talking, it seemed he thought he was up for the remainder of the season. Who knew, maybe he had been told something by the coaching staff and he was sticking with the first team. Once he found out that I was single, he kept steering the conversation towards his exploits with the ladies, which I found a little boorish until Sasha walked past.

"Hey! Hey, Sasha! Over here! How old are you? Thirty? You're quite hot. Do you have any friends who might like Peter here? Don't worry buddy, we'll get you laid."

I was mortified. Sasha seemed more amused than insulted.

"Sorry Sasha, let me talk to Mikhail here alone for a second, would you?" I bundled him into one of the meeting rooms where we could talk alone. "What the hell was that?" I actually had to pause to see which one of the many wrong things he had said that I would address first. "You don't ask a woman how old she is and you don't mention how good looking she is in a work context..." I trailed off as I came to a conclusion. I had worked in office jobs for a while where a certain level of neutering had occurred in all conversations. So for me, it was a no brainer that you removed all of that sort of language from work conversations. But Mikhail? He had never been in an office work environment. His job was that of a hockey player and hockey players learn their behavior in the changing rooms. So he was being as much of a hockey player as he knew how to be but that was all bravado and innuendo.

"Mikhail, you owe Sasha an apology."

He was confused. "Why? I said that she was hot. Too old for me, though, right?"

"Look, you can't talk to women like that. How hot she is or isn't is none of your business. And that shouldn't come into your conversation with her. You just can't say that."

"Why not?"

"Because nobody needs to know your opinion of how hot they are."

That seemed to really throw him. I felt like shaking him.

"Chill, man. We'll get you all hooked up. You just stick with old Mikhail here and before you know it, you'll be fighting them off with a stick."

Like water off a duck's back, my admonishments seemed to have no effect and he wandered out of the office and back into the facility.

It didn't end there though. Not long after that, I got called into Coach's office.

"Take a seat. We've heard about an incident and wanted to get your side of the story."

So I told him what Mikhail had said and what I had said.

"Look, Peter, you've got to show leadership to the team. The kids look up to you. You're in a position of authority and you have to model the sort of behavior that we've come to expect on this team."

I cocked my head. "I thought that's what I had done by calling out his actions and taking him into the office."

Coach continued. "We're just lucky that Sasha isn't interested in making a big deal about this."

And now I frowned. "Are we? Look, if I was supposed to do something else, please let me know what that was."

Coach looked down at a piece of paper on his desk and then I realized he had a script that he was working his way through. "So we'll have to have a session with the team to go through appropriate behaviors."

It really didn't matter what I said in the room. He was following some instructions that HR and/or Legal had put together. For him, success involved getting through the script and then going about his day as usual. I nodded to him and headed back into the training facility, blowing off steam with a hard practice session.

Meeting Ms. Right

The word 'generational' was thrown around to describe the best players in ice hockey. 'A generational talent' meant that you weren't just the best player on your team or the best player in your draft year, but that you were the best player of your whole generation. I could never figure out if a generation in ice hockey was twenty years, ten years or just five. The game certainly changed quickly, every year the board of governors would vote on rule changes and the league itself decided on which rules would be strictly enforced rather than used as loose guidelines. Either way, with the suit, I was a generational talent. And along with my current salary, the envy of any working man or programmer. With a projected salary of truly stupendous numbers came opportunities. A lot of opportunities. My agent may have been trying to put together sponsorship and promotional deals that would pay me handsomely but he was also earning his fee by fielding invitations and requests for my time in social settings.

C. G. Lambert

When it was confirmed that I was single, he told me that the number of invitations spiked. We're talking about invites to balls, art collection openings, costume parties, sports events and fundraisers. They were from magazines, newspapers, TV channels, charities and rich folk with nothing better to do.

I got my agent to put all of the invitations onto a spreadsheet we both had access to. Each week, I would go through the next batch of invitations and check them against our schedule and my other obligations to see which were possible: those I wanted to attend and those that required 'Peter is sorry that he will not be attending your social event, all the best.' It got so bad that my agent had to take on an intern just to handle the volume of invitations.

It was supposed to be a fundraising event for a children's charity and so the entrance to the historic train station had been choked with photographers and red carpet. There was even a crowd of the public held back by barricades and security guards. It was the place to be seen, the social event of the season. A line of limos were parked, ejecting their cargo at the front doors for a red-carpet photo-op, and I couldn't be bothered with that. Besides, while my Uber was perfectly serviceable, it certainly stood out amongst the sleek black limos and town cars being used by the other guests. Instead, I walked along the pavement, skirted around the block and came to the station from one of the other directions. I figured that one of the other doors would give me more direct access and avoid the chaos out front.

I pretty soon found the tradesman's entrance, a gate manned by a security guard armed with a clipboard and a frown. A delivery truck was just leaving and I took the opportunity to slide through the gate. The guard saw me, of course, and yelled out. I turned, not really sure of my next move. I mean, I had an invite, I just didn't want to be forced to go in through the front door and the crowds.

"It's okay, he's one of ours." I heard a woman's voice call out. The security guard looked up and saw what I did, an attractive woman in a suit walking towards us. "You're late, come inside." I shrugged at the security guard and meekly followed her into a loading dock, empty except for a large blue bin and a stack of cardboard boxes. "May I see your invite?" she asked me as we paused. "I assume from the way you're dressed that you've been invited?"

I wordlessly handed it over. She looked at it briefly, handed it back and beckoned for me to follow her. I pocketed it and dutifully followed her through the bowels of the station, past a steady stream of waiters heading in both directions. The ones in the direction we were going had full trays, the ones coming past us had empty trays.

C. G. Lambert

It was very telling, the looks on the faces of those bringing back their empty trays. Most smiled, some nodded at her, but the women next to me was getting a lot of respect. Eventually, we popped out in the main concourse of the station. She inclined her head with a glint in her eye and what could only be described as a smirk on her lips. I nodded my thanks and walked out past the stage just as the band started to play some concerto or overture or fugue, and all eyes involuntarily flicked in my direction. As I was recognized, there was a ripple of reaction and whispering and I subconsciously wiped my face just in case there was any food on it. At a loss for what to do, I made my way over to the drinks table.

There were about a hundred people in a train station that could have held ten times that. Throughout the room mixed and mingled the great and the good. I recognized actors and actresses, captains of industry, other sports notables and media figures. The men in some variation of tuxedos or smart dinner suits and the women in something sheer or sparkly or both.

I nursed a glass of sparkling water while looking around the room. I knew where the wait staff were coming out, where the musicians were and where the table with all the lots were being auctioned off. I maneuvered myself closer to the door to the kitchens and worked out the best place to stand. While the waiters and waitresses all came out of the same set of doors, they fanned out to work all areas of the room. I wanted to be close enough to the doors to be passed by as many of them as possible but without it being obvious that's what I was doing. I had seen the size of the portions of food and knew I would need a fair few servings to get even close to being full.

I mingled a little with various bankers and lawyers and their significant others, excusing myself whenever one of the wait staff came by to get a taste of whatever they were carrying. Eventually there were speeches and general exaltation to bid on one or other of the prizes in the silent auction.

I wasn't paying much attention to the other guests really, just focusing on getting enough food to make the night worthwhile and planning my exit so I could have enough time in bed before the following night's game. But apparently some of the guests had managed to pack away a lot more drinks in the few hours that I had been there. More than maybe their metabolism had been able to handle, anyway.

I saw a kerfuffle out of the corner of my eye, heard raised voices and the choked anger of someone having a disagreement while also trying to keep their voices down to avoid attracting attention. That always had the opposite effect in my experience. As I got closer, I could see that a couple of the older guests were being accosted by the manager who had walked me inside when I had arrived.

"... Oh, I trust my staff when they report these sorts of things. I'm afraid your husband has been behaving poorly and so you should both accompany me to await the police."

The wife was having none of it. You could only describe her body language as 'cornered badger'. She wasn't going anywhere without a fight. "Bertrand would never act inappropriately. Your waitress must be mistaken," she hissed.

"Don't you know who I am? I'm a partner at the biggest law firm in this city. And I take my reputation being damaged very seriously." He was turning a very deep shade of crimson and his jowls were wobbling very threateningly.

The manager wasn't having any of it. "I'm glad we're both taking these accusations so seriously. People like you stop me from being able to offer a safe workplace to my staff, so I'm very keen on removing you both from the vicinity. If you'd like to follow me, we can do this out of the public gaze. We wouldn't want this to be a news story, now would we?"

I was impressed by her control of the situation, her strength of spirit and how she was sticking up for her employees. In the brighter light of the venue, I could tell that she was strikingly attractive. Auburn hair in a sensible ponytail and not a lot of makeup. She must have been in her late thirties, maybe even the same age as me. As she strode off followed by the muttering and spluttering couple, I made my way to the bar and topped up my drink. While the bartender sorted my drink out, I grilled him on the manager.

I found out that Alex was a divorcee who had built up the catering company from scratch over ten years and was very much respected by the staff. I realized that he could have been painting a rosy picture of her just in case his opinions were reported back but he seemed genuine. I even asked if she was dating anyone but he professed ignorance of that. I did get the company name from him though. As I left the venue, I pondered if it would ever work between us. Caterers must be up all hours with their work, surely? And I had the most random of schedules; weeks with no days off and then the complete summer off. Well, not off, but with a strict training regime and no 9-to-5 commitments. Would those schedules ever work? I decided to find out.

It was surprisingly easy to find her work email address and I spent the miserable flight to our next away game trying to figure out the right way to ask her out. Eventually, I kept it simple and said that I had seen her at the event and asked if she wanted to get a frozen yogurt on the weekend. Cliche maybe, but I had no idea what people my age did for dating.

She came back with a yes but that she had work that evening so would have to leave early. Result!

I was maybe five minutes early and waited outside the apartment block for the minutes to tick by before I realized that it made me look like a stalker. She buzzed me into the complex and I found her apartment. She let me in, gave me a peck on the cheek and explained how she was still getting ready and that I should make myself at home on the couch in the lounge. She disappeared upstairs somewhere and I settled onto the couch. The place was tidy. Not show-room ready but not a mess either. A bookshelf with a range of books and board games and photos scattered among them. I was about to be nosey and go and check out the bookshelf when I heard a high-pitched teenager's voice.

"Mom? When are you going out?" More yelled than asked and from the depths of the apartment, so I didn't know if it was upstairs or on the level I was on.

"What did you say the guy's name was?" A pause. I think the girl knew someone was in the lounge and just assumed that it was her mother.

"So sketchy. Does he know how old you are?" She wasn't waiting for answers so this kind of one-sided conversation must be common.

"Peter Collins? What kind of name is that? What does he do? Have you Googled him? I bet he sells real estate. He sounds like he sells real estate." I couldn't hear the keyboard tapping but I knew she must have been checking me out.

"Does he know about your business? Don't tell him how much you pay yourself. You don't want no gold digger." Another pause.

"Did you know there's a Peter Collins that's an ice hockey player?"

In the silence that followed, Alex came down dressed as she had for the gala event. "I hope you don't mind, I'll have to go straight to work afterwards so… Julie, come out and meet Peter."

From the hallway came a teenager with a laptop balanced in front of her. She stopped when she saw me and frowned as if she couldn't believe what her eyes were telling her. "Say hi," prompted her mother.

"… Hi….," she said slowly. "I'm Julie, nice to meet you. What do you do for a living, Peter?"

Alex glanced sharply at Julie at that and seemed about to say something, so I stepped in. "I'm a professional athlete."

Alex did a double take and Julie gave me a disbelieving look. "No, really, I am."

Julie clicked something on her computer and then held it up, looking from it to me and back again. Alex came up behind her and they synchronized head bobs as their brains eventually believed what their eyes were telling them.

"Shall we go?" I asked, ignoring the conversation occurring between mother and daughter by way of semaphore eyebrows.

The Trade Deadline

Getting into a good rhythm is super important and when things are working, you end up just tweaking things around the edges. I was so engrossed in the process that I didn't even notice how far through the season we were. That was until I noticed Benoit, one of our young players in the weight room at the training facility. He was sitting on the bench press machine and staring at his feet. Sometimes players would rest between sets and stare like that but this was different. I was finishing up on the treadmill and so wiped down the machine and stopped by on my way past.

"Everything okay, Benoit?"

"Hmm? Oh, hi Peter. Yeah, just getting in some reps."

"Yeah okay, well... I'll be in the dining room grabbing a snack if you want to chat about anything."

I grabbed a smoothie from the machine and an apple from the dish and settled in to look at my phone. A few seconds later, he slumped into the seat opposite mine.

"Hey."

"Hey, actually, do you have a minute?"

"Sure, what's up?"

"Look, the press is full of stories about me being traded and it's kind of getting to me."

I blinked. Very quickly I thought about the date - we were getting close to the trade deadline.

"I wouldn't have thought you would have anything to worry about. Surely we're doing well enough to be buyers rather than sellers?"

"Yeah, that's what I was thinking too. But the word on the street is that instead of trading draft picks, we should package me up with a couple of prospects to get someone else. I haven't had the best season but I haven't gone backwards. I really want to stay with the team and it's getting to me."

"Shit that's no good. I had no idea."

"Yeah. Would you be able to have a word with the GM? Get a feel for whether I should be worried?"

I looked at him with half a bite of apple sitting unchewed in my mouth. He was young. Really young. Did he really think that a GM would take kindly to that sort of questioning?

"Uh... look, I'm not going to talk to the GM. And I don't think you or anyone else should try to talk to him about it either."

He looked disappointed and like he might try to argue his point, so I held up a hand. "No, listen. I know I haven't been in the league long but I'll tell you something for nothing. If he is trying to make a trade and is negotiating the details, then he can't share that with you because the trade might not come off and then he's told you that you're expendable. What's that going to do to you for the rest of the regular season, let alone the playoffs? But more importantly, this is a business. Don't get me wrong, I love this team and love having you and all the guys here. We're doing good work. We're having success. Winning is fun, right?"

He nodded.

"But it's a business. Coach could decide that I'm not pulling my weight, or he and I could have a difference of opinion and he decides that I'm not needed on the team, and he goes and has a word with the GM. Or the GM could be given a package that he can't say no to. Five first round picks and a prospect or two. That would set the team up for a decade, right? Even if they choose some stinkers in the draft, if you have five additional shots in the first round plus your own five picks, some of those have to be stars, right? So if you could get all of that for just little old me, then maybe he pulls the trigger. I have to be ok with that."

I pointed at him with my water bottle. "You've got an apartment, right? Renting?" A slow nod. "Girlfriend?" Nod. "Kids?" A shake. "Cool. So you have nothing holding you here. If you did get traded, it will be strange but guess what? That's part of the deal. You have to be able to drop everything and go. It's part of being a professional. You don't have to like it and you don't want it to happen. I don't know what I would do if my name was in the press but why the hell are you reading the press?"

"It kind of just happened and now I keep searching for my name and it appears a lot."

"Right. The trade deadline is where everyone is trying to strengthen their team for the playoffs and for the teams who can't make the playoffs to try and get the biggest return on the players who are coming to the end of their contracts. So there's a flurry of activity and every armchair GM has a theory of what the gap is for their team. What deal would address that shortcoming?"

"So many deals!"

"Yeah. Tell you what. You know how you can focus on the game when you're playing it? You've trained yourself to ignore the fight with your girlfriend or parents or whatever's happening off-ice and just switch your brain to hockey mode and think about the game, and your shift, and what you're doing now on the ice?"

"Yeah"

"Well, I think it would help you to do the same thing for this. You have to stay off the socials and definitely don't Google yourself. It'll drive you mad."

"Thanks man. I'll try."

"Hang on, I haven't finished. You know this is my first season, right?"

He looked at me wryly. "Yeah, it's come up a little bit."

"So I know a bunch in theory and how things should be but that might not help you much. So do me a favor. Have a chat with Dr Smith."

"The psych? I don't want them to bench me for being a psycho."

"I don't know why they would bench you. Nah, that's what they pay him for and they might have some more techniques to help you cope. I'm not a doctor or a psychologist. But thanks for coming to me with this. Let me know how you get on with the Doc." I paused for a second "Do you think anyone else is having a hard time? I try to stay off the forums so I don't know what people are saying. Is anyone else feeling the pinch?"

"I think maybe Russell."

"Okay. Keep an ear out for anyone else who might need a chat. I don't know if I've been helpful at all but you're always welcome to my opinion. It might not be right but I'll always try to help."

"Ah well, thanks for listening anyways. I was in two minds about talking to you about it."

"Anytime man."

After my snack, I headed back for the rest of my workout. While doing bicep curls with the second lightest weights, I thought about the trade deadline. I was pretty confident that I wasn't at risk of being traded. I was breaking records left and right. We were winning. We were definitely going to make the playoffs. The back-office staff would be looking at our current roster to try to see what players they could add to bolster our chances at the Cup. Even adding some depth players would be an acceptable move. Doing nothing would be career suicide. If we were knocked out at any stage and had not made any moves, then it would be seen as being because we didn't add any more players. If we won, then whatever moves management made would be seen as being acts of genius. Adding players coming to the end of their contracts were termed rentals because you got them as players for maybe three months from March to June and then they would be Unrestricted Free

Agents, free to negotiate with any team for the next season. So giving up prospects and draft choices could be an expensive way of improving the team. That draft choice might end up being a superstar and if you've given it up for a few months for a player who in the end is not going to move the needle, then you could get accused of mortgaging the team's future. Many a GM has faced a steady stream of seasons where they continually make the playoffs and tried to improve at the trade deadline only to have seen their stock of draft picks slowly deteriorate.

So maybe as a result of arrogance, I was pretty sure the team wouldn't trade away such a central reason for this season's success. The other players might not be as secure. It was definitely possible to upgrade any position and that might mean being the player traded away to get a slightly better player. If the team had an obvious position of weakness, the GM might trade away someone from a position that they had too much depth in to rectify that position of weakness.

We were on the road a couple of days before the trade deadline and one of the younger guys in the team was approached by one of the assistant managers on the plane when we were nearing our destination. I saw the reaction of the player and then the assistant manager walked back down the aisle. I went over and the player was sitting in his chair, with a shocked look on his face.

"Everything okay, Grant?"

He looked up at me in surprise. "I've been traded."

"Ah bugger. Where to?"

He told me. "And who for?"

He told me the players involved. "Well, at least they've traded you for a guy in your position."

He looked up at me, confused. So I clarified. "Well, you play forward, right? So if they traded you for a defenseman or a goalie, that would mean that they would have one more forward than they used to have, so there would be a greater chance of you being the extra player that they don't need to dress for the next games. But if you get swapped for another forward, then at least there's a hole for you to slot into and it looks like the hole might be higher on the roster because they've packaged you with some draft picks. So you might even make it onto their second or third line. Silver linings!"

He looked a little more relaxed than when I had first approached him. "Maybe. But what am I going to tell my girlfriend?"

I shook my head. "This is the job, man. If she didn't know that going in, then she will now. All the best though. It was good playing with you."

The Forty Year Old Rookie

He wasn't the only one traded away. Our GM had been working the phones and had put together a number of trades designed to get us in a better position for the playoffs. We lost two of the guys on the first team in exchange for a player coming to the end of his contract, and another one with a lot more term on his contract who had proven himself to be a bargain for his abilities. I could already see the GM making moves to accommodate my huge salary the next season. One eye on the now and one on the future.

The Playoffs

There are some leagues where the players make a point of showing how tough they are. They maybe don't have the skill or the technique to make it in the bigs and so have to prove themselves with their toughness. I don't mean those who reluctantly fight because that's how they add value to their team, I'm talking about players who run players from behind, stir shit up by running the goalie, seeking out players to hurt, that sort of thing. When all the players are professionals, you can see how they might be conflicted. Because in these leagues, they're not getting paid the big bucks. We're talking sub-$50k mostly. These are the guys that will try and take your head off without the promise of a Stanley Cup or a million-dollar deal in the majors at stake. And so it's natural for the other professionals to look sideways at this. There's a respect among the highest professional leagues - you don't want to hurt anyone, not really, because you know that they might have a wife and kids to support. And if you come into a check slightly wrong, you can hurt someone pretty badly and they can be out of the lineup for a long time. Sometimes players don't ever come back from an injury and even if insurance covers a contract, if you're coming to the end of your entry level contract, a career-ending injury represents a lot of money left on the table. This respect was writ large in Gretzky's last season when players would warn him that they were coming for a check. Nobody wanted to appear on Wikipedia as the reason why the Great One ended his playing days.

Except in the playoffs. If you don't want to hurt anyone in the regular season because you're all playing the game as a job, all that goes out the window when the playoffs begin. Then every injury which forces an opposing player out of the playoffs makes their team weaker and makes your path to the Cup that much easier.

Looking back on my little adventure, a lot of the conversations I had occurred in a bar, over a beer. While the volume of alcohol in the professional leagues had reduced significantly over the years, hockey remained a social game and having a quiet few beverages after a game wasn't the sole privilege of the beer leaguers.

We were on the road having completed the end of our regular season. The Presidents' Trophy was in the bag, and the last few teams jostled for the final wild card slots. We had a favorable series of road trip games and ended up with an extra day between them.

Naturally enough, we headed out for a quiet drink, finding ourselves at a bar not incredibly far from the hotel. The various games were showing around the league on big screen TVs around the walls of the bar and we settled into a bunch of the booths, six or seven per booth.

One screen showed a fight and that naturally attracted the attention of the guys.

"Who was that?"

"That's Pritchard. He's been bouncing around in one of the lower leagues and they signed him mid-season because their team is too soft. Talk about an overreaction. The guy's a caveman!"

"Where did he play?"

"A real bush league - fights in the penalty boxes, players climbing into the stands, stick fights, the whole thing."

"And he got called up into the NHL?"

A shrug. "I guess their team got tired of being pushed around."

"It won't end well," opined Pers, one of our Swedes. "It's one thing when a player can fight or if you call up an enforcer from the AHL. At least you know that they can skate and play, and they won't be looking to actually hurt anyone."

That got a wry grin from one of the rookies. "All the guys I see in fights look like they're trying to hurt the other guy."

Pers shook his head. "You know what I mean. Sure, in the playoffs, all bets are off but in the regular season, you know the other guy is there earning a living, supporting their family. I mean, you're still trying to play hard and fast and take the body but except for a very few exceptions, you're not actually trying to hurt people out there."

"Except those real dirty players, right? They're always looking for a slew foot, or a knee-on-knee or a blindside hit. But you know those guys and periodically they'll get tagged up because you can't run from the ramifications of your actions forever."

"So the majority of players aren't trying to hurt people?" asked Stan.

"Haha, while I agree with that in principle, wasn't there that goalie that got run over and had to leave the game?" I asked, referring to Pers in a previous season.

"Yeah, that was an accident. I blew a tire and ran straight into him. Took his knee out because he couldn't dodge me in time and I was sliding so I couldn't do anything about that."

"Yeah, sure, but either way, it meant their backup came in and he stonewalled you guys for the rest of the series. In hindsight, it's almost like you would have been better with their number one goalie."

"You sound like the press. But that's not the way anyone thinks on the ice. You play hard. Very hard. You need an edge. And you'd do anything to get that edge, to win the puck, to win the shift, to score the goal, to win the game."

I looked around the bar. To a man, every single one of them had played close to twenty years of ice hockey, some of them thirty. Whether they were in their rookie year or were coming to the end of their career, they had a set of skills which were by no means unique. While you could measure their speed or how fast their wrist or slap shot was or how accurate they could shoot, with or without traffic and against this or that goalie, what I realized then that the coaching and scouting staff were looking for was that 'do anything for the team' attitude. It wasn't a secret. It appeared constantly in interviews, in print, and in person. But here, in a booth in a bar surrounded by my teammates, listening to their stories, I finally got it.

That made me so very grateful not to have to fight. Think about it. A judge is a judge because they can objectively weigh up the evidence, decide on guilt and then apply judgment. If you don't think in terms of objective justice, you're just arranging things in your favor. You're a dictator. But if you don't think about objective justice, then your coach and teammates will look at you funny because you're putting justice and impartiality above your own team. You really do have to be a rabid 'team first' player. And having the suit put me in the singular position that I could rain down retribution on the players who wronged my team. Regardless of whether the transgressors, in the cold light of day, really deserved such treatment.

Now one thing they don't tell you is that you don't get paid in the playoffs. The team gets hotel rooms regardless if the next game is home or away. Since you're at the team hotel, you don't get a full per diem. That means that you might not get paid enough to pay for your lunch and dinner. I had saved my money because I wasn't living high on the hog enough to need it but I saw one or two of the young guys starting to tighten their belts. They called them the Black Aces. They're the guys who are on the roster and practice separately to keep their skills up but they won't get a game unless someone gets hurt. The trainers make sure to keep pushing them hard but they have a miserable existence, hoping that one of the first team gets hurt so then they can get playoff game time.

The problem is that they have outgoings that don't stop just because they're staying in a hotel. They have their apartment near the AHL team's arena or training facility. They have water, power, gas, internet and all of the regular outgoings that you normally have and they're not getting paid. They would normally be paying the bills with their AHL salary but since that was so low, they might not have been saving enough to get by in the off-season. And since they were on standby for the playoffs, they couldn't get a summer job to earn extra money.

One of them figured out that they could scalp their tickets to make a few extra bucks. Each player got a couple of tickets to each game and if you sold two tickets at a face value of $300-400, that got you $700 in the hand. When you're getting $50 as a per diem and have to eat out for lunch and dinner, that goes a long way towards not going backwards in the old bank account.

You do get paid in the payoffs as a bonus payment depending on how far you make it, anything from $11k for first round, $22k for the second round, $54k for the third round, $98k if you lose the final and $163k if you win the Cup. That said, these numbers change year to year, and get this - the league actually gives the team a pot of money and it's up to the team how they split that amongst the players. So if they decide that only the players who play a game in the playoffs get a share, then you could have been one of the Black Aces, practicing hard and staying away from your family for three or four weeks, trying to live on $50 a day and still not get anything.

Winning the Stanley Cup is a year-long pursuit which journalists anecdotally call a 'road' or a 'journey.' The regular season is an eighty-two-game grind which ends when 16 teams qualify and then the postseason or playoffs begin. Four rounds of best of seven series ending with the crowning of the champions. It was a source of much debate among the journalists looking for something to write about. Does momentum from the regular season carry into the playoffs? Do hot streaks continue? Does what you've learned about the opposition matter in the post-season? A lot has been written about this.

I'm here to tell you that nothing matters. It is literally a clean slate. Nobody knows anything. None of your performances matter. Nothing matters except getting to sixteen wins before you lose four against any one opponent. Players play through injuries. You find out after the playoffs are over who played on a broken ankle or with broken ribs. In the regular season, those injuries are announced. In the playoffs, that is intelligence that could be weaponized. Team depth is tested. The ability for coaches to determine the best approach against any opponent and to make changes in-game is crucial. How the team reacts to being behind on the scoreboard.

C. G. Lambert

How the star players react to the closer checking. How the team shuts down the opponent's star players. How you handle the mismatched scheduling when one team has progressed while their opponent is still playing, so the rest periods don't align.

We finished the regular season with the best record and so we won the Presidents' Trophy. It was the most double-edged sword in professional ice hockey. The trophy was supposed to celebrate the success you had in the regular season but ever since they limited how much a team could spend on player's salaries, the winners had gone on to win the Stanley Cup only twice in over twenty years. So less than ten percent. If success was random, you'd have a one in sixteen chance of winning the Cup. Six and a bit percent. So the teams which won the Presidents' Trophy won the Stanley Cup about one and a half times more often than just some random team. This meant that winning the Presidents' Trophy was definitely an indicator of how good the team was but put another way, teams who had not won the Presidents' Trophy won the Stanley Cup nineteen times in twenty-one years. Or close to 90%.

The fact that you were nine times as likely to win the Stanley Cup if you didn't win the Presidents' Trophy suggested to me that the attributes celebrated by the Presidents' Trophy - a team learning what it takes to win games in the regular season, coaches putting systems into place and players buying onto those systems - are all useless in the postseason. Run a magnet over your brain. Ctrl-A, Delete. Nothing matters.

I finished the season with the Maurice Richard Trophy for scoring the most goals in the season and the Selke for having the best plus/minus. I finished the regular season with the best points record ever in league history. Award after award. Whenever a journalist would gush about this record or that record, I would shake my head. "None of that matters. We're into the playoffs and now we have to relearn how to win."

"But surely on a personal level, you must be happy with your performance in the regular season?"

"I'm not being falsely modest. None of it matters. We secured our playoff position and our coach will get the last change because we get home team advantage because we won the Presidents' Trophy. If we don't win the Stanley Cup, then it's just a Wikipedia entry. Someone else will break my personal records someday. But what will be remembered is who wins the Cup this year."

"Do you have any bonuses tied to your performance in the regular season?"

"I'm not even going to check. My mind is purely on the next game. I'm not giving any bandwidth to anything else."

"Seriously? You scored—"

"Any other questions?"

"What do you think about the rules stopping you from being eligible for the Calder Cup as best rookie of the year?"

"I don't care." The reporters seemed shocked by such a response.

"But surely it would be good to get that trophy to go along with all of the others in your trophy case?"

"I'm not sure any of you understand what I'm saying. I've trained myself to do two things: focus on the next game and switch off from hockey entirely, which allows me to be able to go back to focusing on the next game with more intensity. I apologize that none of my answers to your questions are going to be satisfactory until the playoffs are over. So any questions about personal records, league records, contracts or bonuses are all going to be at best ignored and at worst... well... Let's just say it might not be a good idea to push them. If I had my way, I'd have a total embargo, so then we wouldn't have any questions at all but that obviously wouldn't be fair on you guys. We'll keep coming up with answers but do me a favor? Keep the questions short and I'll try to get you enough for your stories."

The Forty Year Old Rookie

The collected throng of reports didn't quite look like kicked puppies but the easy going and very open Peter they had been dealing with was now replaced by a very taciturn and stern Peter.

345

Our Playoffs

We won the first round through habit. We were still firing on all cylinders and our opponent had only just squeaked into the last wild card slot for the playoffs, securing their spot on the last day of the regular season. For them, that was the achievement for the year, so we swept them in four games.

I was still playing in the suit, regardless of my experience playing without it in that one game. I didn't believe that I had played a whole game, dominated a game actually, without it. Sure, I was feeling good in general and I was fitter than I had ever been, but I never expected that to translate into actual ability. Best not to try that again. Just in case it was a fluke.

In the second round, we came across a team who had a superstar in goal and they were peaking at just the right time. So we had to dig pretty deep to get past them. We were lucky that their coaching staff didn't do a good enough job keeping me under control, and so I was able to slip defenders and find my linemates with passes.

Even though their goalie stood on his head, Coach double shifted me at the right times and I found the right players in the right spots to get some scoring. But we were winning games 3-2 and 2-1 and out shooting them 45-15. Their goalie was just that good. We still swept them but only just, and one of the games went into overtime.

The third round was actually easier. Their team did a much better job of marking me but their goalie was nowhere as good as the one in the second round. So while I was double teamed and suffered cross checks and hacks to unprotected parts of the anatomy, when we got in their zone, we were able to put the puck away. We only dropped one game in that series. Everyone has a bad game at some time or another.

Which put us in the finals! Four wins away from lifting the Stanley Cup. The dream of any kid growing up playing ice hockey. The chance to get your name etched onto the Cup to join the legendary players who had won it in the past.

Our opponents? Another elite team who had been to the finals the previous three seasons. Again, a great goalie playing well, and again great coaching staff making smart decisions. We split the first four games, each team winning one game at home and another on the road. Back and forth we went and I remembered being in the lounge of the team hotel after the last loss, sitting in an armchair looking out the window at the rain early in the morning because I couldn't sleep. The scenes from the game were still bouncing around my head.

That was where I had my epiphany. It was so obvious, it was shameful. Ice hockey was a team sport. Team sports are not about any one player, regardless of how good they are. I was thinking about the settings in the programming for my suit. If I put them all - balance, speed, stopping - at 100, then that wouldn't matter to the outcome of the game. Even if I put them at 110, it wouldn't matter. Because the thing that mattered was finding that extra gear. For all the players on the team.

That's why winning the Presidents' Trophy was so double-edged. Winning it proved that you could win during the regular season. Not only could you win but it proved that you could win a lot when the games mattered a little and when the stakes were a slot in the playoffs. But it didn't prove that you could will yourself to win when your survival was on the line. It didn't show that your coach knew how to outcoach the opposition when the games mattered. Winning the Presidents' Trophy didn't show that the players knew how to collectively focus on that game, that shift, that stride, so closely as to make it their entire world for that particular minute or thirty seconds or however long it took. Forgetting about the crowd, the fans, the TV crews, their friends and their family, and their wife or girlfriend or parents.

That's why the team that won the Stanley Cup very frequently lost the finals the year before or maybe had bowed out in the Conference finals. They had learned that their best wasn't good enough and they learned by watching the team that beat them to see how the opposition had dug deeper than they could.

That night, I realized that winning the Stanley Cup wouldn't be about me. It couldn't be about me - it would always be about the team. And the team's ability to find that extra gear.

So in the changing room before the start of game five, I did something I had never done all season. I stood up and made a speech. I went around the room and said a few words about each of the guys and what they meant to me. A little vignette about each of them. Coach and the captains all stood by watching and the team went out onto the ice in good spirits. You could feel how they wanted to perform for each other and for me. We got smoked. We went down 5-1.

I was lucky not to get a suspension because I lost my composure on the ice. One too many fifty/fifty calls went against us and I let my exasperation show. That didn't cause the loss - we were already

4-1 down when I got a little bit shouty. The refs didn't like being called out like that and gave me two minutes for unsportsmanlike behavior. All season long, I had held my tongue when the calls had gone against us. All season long, I had cultivated a reputation with the referees as someone who maybe asked about a penalty or a non-call but wouldn't do it to try and gain an advantage or make them look bad. Merely to learn. A respectful player.

But all that went out the window when it looked like I would be sitting for most of the rest of the game and that would mean whatever slim chance of a comeback dried up faster than a sliver of spittle on a griddle. They let me have it - adding on a 10-minute game misconduct. Some people take notice of a statistic called Net Penalties Drawn which compares how many times you put your team down a man because of a penalty you took versus how many times you managed to get one of the opposition players penalized. That was the first game where I had a negative net Penalties Drawn and the first time I had put my team at a disadvantage because of my actions. I got kicked out of the game with about three minutes left and stomped off the ice to the changing rooms.

It was a very long three minutes and an even longer evening. Thankfully, Coach didn't dwell for too long on the game, on our effort or the results and we went straight to the hotel afterwards.

But not before facing the press. Whereas after each game in the regular season you might have a knot of reporters in the changing room asking questions, in the playoffs, after each game there was a full-on press conference in a special room with lights and a packed gallery.

The media manager for the team asked me if I'd attend and so I dutifully followed Coach out to the table at the end of the room and sat while he fielded a couple of soft questions to start the night off. Then it was my turn.

"What was the big disagreement out there? Was it the trip on O'Reilly?"

"Yeah, I lost my cool on that missed call and went too far with the ref. I was feeling frustrated and our opponents had done a really good job on playing close to the line. It seemed like every call was going against us."

"You'd done such a good job during the season of keeping your emotions in check so it was actually a relief to see you show some passion out there."

I felt my temper rising and took a second or two before answering. "Um, no. I'm always passionate about the game, even in the regular season. I'm not worried about being emotional on the ice but one thing I am sorry about is getting called for that penalty because even two or three goals down, you feel like coming back might be an achievable target. But you can't score from the penalty box and you definitely can't score from the changing rooms."

"Coach, are you happy with the refereeing so far?"

"We didn't get the result we were looking for. It's the Stanley Cup final. Both teams are going to try and find any advantage and they did a fantastic job of skating close to the edge. You could argue that a few of their checks were late but these are the playoffs. You could argue that some of the extracurricular activity crossed the line but again, these are the playoffs. This is the finals."

"What's the plan now?"

"We're going to go back to the hotel. In the morning, we'll travel and then we'll have a light practice before game six."

I was expecting someone on the coaching staff to give me a hard time or to say something like "You cost us the game" but none of them did. I guess there would be no point in doing that. We needed me at the top of my game and beating me up for something that was arguably not my fault probably wasn't the right approach. I had certainly played in a few teams where that's exactly what someone would have said. Either to your face or behind your back.

Game six was in the opposing team's arena and we were staring elimination in the face. We'd had a light practice and the only ramification from the game that was discussed was around how to keep our discipline in those rucks and scrums that happened after whistles, and to keep focusing on our game. If the only thing that they could do to win was to disrupt and to spoil our flow, then we would have to double down and block those things out. We certainly wouldn't back down but we would play twice as hard.

Seeing the success that they had with me in game five, our opposition doubled down in an attempt to get me off my game. But this time, it actually worked against them. When the rat on a team stirs up trouble, he knows how to go about it to avoid detection while maximizing the chance of riling their opponent up. When everyone is trying to do the same thing, you get players who would never dream of slashing someone trying to get away with it right in front of the ref. So it was only a matter of time before we started to get the benefit of the doubt.

About halfway through the first period, the refs couldn't avoid noticing a flagrant two-handed swing at my ankles, so we found ourselves on a powerplay. We didn't convert on it but the momentum continued afterwards and on my next shift, there was a scrum after the whistle and again, the correct calls were made and two of their guys ended up in the bin along with only one of ours, all for roughing. This time, we made them pay even though the final shot only went in off their defenseman who was trying to block the shot and caught enough of it to change the puck's direction, which beat the goalie. After that, you could see their coach try to rein in the 'after the whistle' activities but it didn't stop the more skillful of their antagonists from having a go if they thought they could get away with it.

I tried to see where that scrutiny might lead to a scoring opportunity and I wasn't disappointed. We were still only one goal up, and the puck was in our zone. Our defenseman had collected it and I had arrived early, so instead of coming down the slot and turning to lead the breakout like I should as the centreman, I had instead placed my butt on the boards at the hashmark, looking for the outlet pass. Their forecheckers pressured the puck carrier who took advantage of my support, sending me over a pass. By then, the winger who should have been where I was had made it onto the ice and was coming down the middle, looking for the pass to start the attack. I wasted no time sending a sharp pass straight to his stick but the sight of me against the boards having just touched the puck (and therefore being a legitimate target for a check) was too tempting for the opposition and I could see two of them coming to lay the body. I wasn't surprised when I could already see the elbows starting to rise as the players approached. If I hadn't been wearing the suit, then the resulting check would probably have put me in the hospital.

They both left their feet, so they both should have been penalized for charging; one of them led with their stick which should have been called for cross checking and the other one led with his elbow, so there should have been a five minute there for elbowing. Instead, I absorbed the checks and skated to the bench, looking at the refs to see which of the penalties they might call. It turned out that the double teaming had left them short a man in defending the rush and we had scored, so the refs were far more interested in that than giving us a penalty. Once we were up two goals, we circled the wagons and closed them down for the rest of the game. It did mean having to avoid retaliation and turning the other cheek when they realized they had let us back into the series but what had started with us feeling desperation turned into self-belief and then a sense of destiny.

In a game where the margin of success was slim, what should have been a nervous game for us, being on the verge of elimination, ended up in a two-goal margin of victory. The failure to get me off my game distracted them from what had worked previously and got us back to parity in the series. And so it all came down to game seven in the Stanley Cup finals.

The Final

I had learned a lot during my first year playing professional ice hockey. I had learned the sort of lessons that some players never learn in their whole careers. One of those was what was actually required to win in the postseason. I mean, I had watched hockey for a long time and even a blind man could see the statistical change from the regular season to playoffs. Every commentator would say that there was less time and less ice to make plays, that there were more shots blocked, and that the coaching was laser focused on getting the matchups they wanted, tweaking and changing tactics to make sure that star players were countered.

I had even read some people who said that because of all of this, that it really didn't matter who you had on your top two lines, that the Stanley Cup was won by the deepest team. The one where the players who did not have all the kudos and attention - the bottom six forwards and third line defense pair. These were the most important players because they were the ones who would find themselves with the puck and the opportunity to make meaningful plays. That would put the puck in the net because the opponents were too busy running around trying to shut down the superstars. I hadn't done the math to see if that was historically true but I did know that there were always the heroes of the playoffs, the guys who you would not expect to see on the scoreboard who came through in the final series. Or maybe they just stood out because they were the names you did not expect to see on the scoreboard.

Either way, I had come to the conclusion that no matter what settings I had set the suit to, I probably wouldn't be the star of the Finals. I wanted to make sure that the opposition didn't score while I was on the ice but I had slowly come around to the conclusion that a coach and a team who saw me as the biggest threat on the ice would do everything that was possible to ensure that I didn't get the puck and that if I did get the puck, I didn't have any space to make a play. If I chose to shoot, the puck would not get through to the goalie. A no brainer really - everything I would have done if I was the coach. Normally when that happened during the regular season, I would find ways of getting the puck to my linemates, so they could take the shot. But they were doing a wonderful job in taking away time and space for them as well. Total lockdown.

C. G. Lambert

All I could do was make myself hard to play against: to take the body, to forecheck hard and to make sure that they paid a heavy toll in keeping me off the scoresheet. And then all I had to do was hope and pray that the other guys on my team could find a way to get the puck in the net. This must have been how coaches feel. I wanted something so badly but there was nothing I could do myself, so I had to focus on how to get the desired outcome by manipulating the forces available to me. At least in Coach's case, it was the mix of players that he put on the ice. For me, all I could do was to take care of business when I was on the ice and be a good teammate when I was on the bench. It was nerve-wracking. We went down a goal early on a turnover in the neutral zone with one of their snipers who crossed the blue line and used our defenseman as a screen. He got the shot away before the defenseman could close the gap. Bang, straight over the goalie's shoulder. One nil. We got back level not long afterwards off of a brilliant give and go with our second line.

Then our third line started to really hum, cycling the puck in their zone for a good portion of time which ended with a couple of legitimate scoring chances. We could feel the momentum swing in our favor.

The din of the crowd was deafening. They could smell it, the expectation, and hope was palpable. But the whole team was dialed in. It was almost like there was no crowd and no noise - each person was so focused. Coach was pointing at players and giving directions like he was directing traffic. The players were ignoring everything except what was happening on the ice. This level of focus and attention was what the whole season, postseason, and in a lot of cases, the whole of a player's career had been building up to. In that instant, I could see the difference between the other players and myself. While I had made the Stanley Cup my focus for this year, each of the players on the bench, the men behind it and the team of people in the back office behind the scenes had been making the Cup the focus of their lives for longer and on a deeper level. It was humbling.

I went out for shift after shift, skating the hardest I had all season. When I had the puck, I made smart plays and when I didn't, I found space. When they had the puck, I closed down my player. I kept an eye out for 50/50 pucks and loose passes that I could beat opposition players to in order to get an odd man rush, but the opposition were playing with an edge and not making any mistakes. They had researched me and knew how far the puck would need to be away from me for it to be contestable. It was frustrating to say the least but I had to have faith in the team to get over the line. The tension steadily ratcheted up, shift by shift, minute by minute. Backwards and forwards we skated.

When the goal finally came, I was on the bench having just come off a double shift and it happened in the blink of an eye. We had dumped the puck in so that my line could change. Our checking line went out and maybe one of the forwards was on a little earlier than I got off, it was hard to tell. They got on the forecheck quickly, forcing their defenseman to make a hasty pass D to D. Our winger was all over the receiving defenseman and managed to get his stick in between the player and the puck and knock the puck away, right into the slot. This led to the center coming late, cruising down the slot and finding himself unmarked with the puck, with a goalie with one pad against the upright post and half of the net to shoot at. He didn't waste the opportunity and every man on the team was off the bench celebrating. I looked at the scoreboard - ten minutes to go. After the player swung past the bench, Coach sent the next line out, and came up behind me.

"We'll lock them down now. We have to soak up the clock. Get the puck in their zone and keep it there. Kill the puck against the boards. Get it deep and keep it there. They can't score from our zone and they can't pull the goalie if they can't get the puck away."

This goal changed the tactics that the opposition would have to use. Instead of concentrating on me, they would have to focus on themselves. They would have to find a way to generate offense. The good news was that we didn't have to do anything of the sort.

My next shift was the most elated I had felt on the ice all year. I had no pressure at all. All I had to do was skate hard and forecheck. Once we had the puck, all we had to do was make the halfway line and then dump it in. And then I was on them. I chased that puck like a fiend - like a greyhound chasing the mechanical bunny at the races. So often the D-men would retrieve the puck and I would be breathing down their necks. They would make a pass to relieve the pressure but I would stop on a dime and go the other way, closing the space to the puck carrier. They, in turn, would look to formulate some sort of break-out to get the puck out of the zone and transition it into an attack. But with the puck only arriving seconds before I did, it was hard to get that second to make a clear pass to one of the forwards moving up the ice. It must have looked hilarious, as if they were playing keep away from me, but the looks on their faces belied the seriousness of their efforts and how they weren't able to get a controlled outlet going. My wingers were staying high, looking to break any passes that did make it to the forwards breaking out, and for a wonderful few minutes we kept them pinned in their zone. The puck was constantly one step ahead of me but my pace and persistence meant that their whole line was harried and harassed. It was a tribute to their skill and ability that they never coughed the puck up no matter how close I got to it or how hard I tried to separate them from it. Eventually I managed to pin the player with the puck against the boards and keep the puck trapped against the base of the boards.

The refs blew the whistle and it was time to get a change. The guys on the bench were going mental and the sound of the crowd was a wave of white noise. We could smell the victory and so could they. There were only a couple of minutes left in the game and the opposing team's coach called a timeout to get his best players a breath of air and reset them after being pinned in their zone for so long. The face-off would still happen back there and they knew what they needed to do but they needed to stop our momentum and try and wrest control back.

I was huffing and puffing on the bench as I tried to catch my own breath after such an effort on the forecheck, so the two-minute break was appreciated. Coach started our second line and they did a wonderful job of clogging up the neutral zone, preventing any sort of coherent attack. Then he tapped me on the back and I went out for the last shift. They were constantly looking to pull their

The Forty Year Old Rookie

goalie to get another skater on the ice but whenever it looked likely, we managed to get the puck or at least look like we might, so the goalie skated towards the bench and then had to hurry back to their crease. Until it got to the point where needed that extra skater to claw their way back in the game and so the goalie decided to skate to the bench no matter who had the puck.

Karl, our Swedish defenseman, got the puck and shot it the length of the ice but it was off target and I managed to beat their defensemen to it to avoid the icing call. I had sprinted to make the touch but had no interest in getting splatted against the boards behind their goal and so I flew past the puck, made my touch as I went past and then skated back to the center of the blue line and waited for them to collect the puck and make a break out. But they were gassed. They'd given all they could and had been hoping on an icing call to have the time after the whistle to catch their breath. Since I had kept the puck in play, they had to keep skating on tired legs.

When the whistle finally went, I couldn't hear it. I knew it was over when I saw the other team's players stop skating and slump on their bench. Our team came over the boards, flinging their gloves in the air and jumping and leaping. Whooping and hollering and babbling the most incoherent rubbish. We clumped together in pairs and threes, hugging each other and moving onto the next guy, slowly coalescing into a mass of humanity close to the goalie. I looked around at the mostly bearded faces, most guys missing teeth and a lot with long hair, and thought that it was like something out of one of my computer games. One of the medieval ones with armored miscreants with scarred faces, unkempt hair and impressive beards. It was totally overwhelming. The tension of the playoffs and the final series had finally been released and the energy came out as bellowing and yelling as all the pressure and effort of the season culminated in that moment. We had won!

The Aftermath

It was overwhelming, but I tried to take it all in. The handshake line. The Stanley Cup presentation. Our captain handing me the Cup. Skating around the rink holding it aloft and then handing it off to our goalie. Some personal trophies were presented to me and passed immediately to the equipment staff. There was a photo on the ice of all of the team, plus the trainers and coaches, all surrounding the Cup.

Back to the changing rooms and grabbing beers. There was elation. Nobody was in a hurry to remove their gear and get changed, and there was this enormous wave of emotion carrying us all as the night began. Eventually we must have showered and gotten changed, with the press interrupting with demands for answers to questions, which could only be answered in the most mundane ways. I saw one of our veterans trying to answer the obvious question of, "How does it feel to finally win the Cup?" He couldn't answer and I felt like I knew why. He was a thirty-five-year-old coming to the end of his career and getting his first, and most likely, last Stanley Cup. Finally, it had been won after thirty years of dreaming of that goal and his parents had paid the price of getting him to practices, buying gear and then putting him in camps, programs and schools to get him the best opportunity. Then there was the player himself sacrificing everything to get in the gym and on the ice and into teams. Moving cities when he made a youth team or got traded or drafted, and getting married but having to share his life with the game. Missing Christmases, birthdays, births, deaths, anniversaries and training over the summer to be ready for the next season, and dealing with injuries and being sent down to the minors. Then there was each of the playoffs, only to spend months concentrating solely on the next game, and so not being available for his kids, wife or family. Then to finally make it and win it all, and have some guy with a microphone stick it in your face and ask that. How do you sum up that level of dedication and commitment in a thirty second sound bite?

I made sure the equipment guys had the trophies and the suit safely squared away. After a few hours drinking in the changing rooms, we took Lord Stanley's Cup out into the city.

I woke up with a splitting headache in an unfamiliar bed in the team hotel with sunlight streaming through the windows, still fully dressed. As I stumbled to the bathroom to relieve the pressure of my bladder and try to rehydrate, snippets of the previous night's carnage flicked through my memory. I was mid-pee, watching the memory play out over my head, when a voice from the bathtub broke my reverie.

"Quite a night, right?"

I finished up and washed my hands before pulling the curtain to one side. Lying in the bathtub was Mikael. I took a moment to drink from the faucet, cupping my hands and ignoring the cups still in their little plastic bags in front of the mirror before turning to him. "Who's room are we in?"

He looked around at the small bottles of toiletries, the little cardboard boxes holding shower caps, vanity kits and combs, all with the emblem of the hotel chain emblazoned on the classy off-white labels. Nothing personalized, so no indication. "No clue."

I nodded. An unnoticed din was competing with the throbbing vein in my ear for my attention, a party if I was any judge of it. I wandered out towards the noise, down the hall, with the music getting louder and the voices competing with it. I knocked on the door where it was loudest and it swung open, revealing the impressive physique of Tony, our enforcer. "Peter! Great to see you man, come in, we're just starting on the Jack."

I blearily followed him into the suite, and marveled at the chaos within. Three or four of the players were seated on the couches in the lounge area, surrounded by cans and bottles, playing cards on a low coffee table. They all acknowledged me as I made my way through the room. Tony led me past a couple of rooms with the doors wide open and various limbs entangled in bedclothes merely suggesting the number of inhabitants until we got to the master bedroom with an enormous bed. One of the two league mandated Cup monitors was asleep in the corner, still wearing the white gloves he wore when he handled the cup. The other was nowhere to be seen but the trophy itself was in bed and Karl was curled up with it, spooning it like a lover.

Tony turned to me, grabbed me by the shoulders and brought his face near mine. Stale beer and spirits assaulted my nose as he winked at me and conspiratorially whispered, "We won the Cup!" I returned his smile and unsteadily wandered back past the carnage to the hallway. I say carnage but upon reflection, none of the fittings or furnishings were broken. Sure, there was a lot of mess and housekeeping might be cursing our names but there weren't streaks of vomit on the walls or huge puddles of red wine staining carpets anywhere. Say what you like about ice hockey players, they at least could handle their booze. Well, the rest of them could. I shuddered to think how much I had drunk but I figured it couldn't be too much as I was still standing. A little wobbly but still in one piece, and I still had my phone, wallet and keys. I wandered down the hall, figuring I could get some food into my system and start to feel a little more human.

I pressed the button for the ground floor and headed for reception. I half expected the lobby to be filled with road cones and Zambonis or some other evidence of a raucous night on the town after winning the Stanley Cup but there was absolutely no evidence of that at all, just the odd group of tourists waiting with their luggage to check out.

I caught the eye of a staff member and asked where the restaurant was. She pointed further along the ground floor. I meandered my way there and a lovely girl asked me what room number I was. I considered the question for a second, turning it around in my addled brain before shrugging and telling her one of the things that I was sure of. "I'm with the team. We won the Cup!" My beaming smile persuaded her. She made a mark on her list and beckoned me into the breakfast buffet.

I piled up my plate, going heavy on the savory and light on the sweet in an attempt to sop up the alcohol, and settled down with a large orange juice. I nodded to the lady doing the rounds with the coffee and raised an eyebrow at her in a 'Decaf or regular?' question. She got the subtle message.

While I made my way through the foodstuffs, I got out my phone and went through the messages and photos. Soooo many of both. The messages were a timeline of carnage, of group chats coordinating our trip throughout the city. The photos and videos were a study in our adventures across the city. There was the Cup and team in a fountain, on a bridge, at a strip club, at a different strip club, and at so many different sports bars. There were group shots of us with the Cup, with fans, with cops on horses, on motorbikes or on foot. There was shaky camera footage of us running down the street. There were so many selfies. With fans, with ladies, with ladies kissing me on each cheek; it was amazing. I went up for a second helping of food and accepted more coffee. I was starting to feel more alive, although with that curious empty feeling that came after a heavy session of drinking.

After finishing my breakfast, and even with two coffees and a full stomach, I just wanted to crash and catch up on some sleep. I checked my pockets for my key card but I couldn't find anything and in my still-drunk state, decided to head home. I headed back past reception and out into the city. It was eight o'clock in the morning and the city had been up for a long time but it was kind to me as I made my way to the underground and back home. There was a lot of recognition as I noticed that my face was blazoned across the front page of the paper and inside there were a lot of photos from our win. I got a fair few high fives and even some of our team chants started up on the platforms as I waited to transfer lines. I grinned along with them and shook hands but my headache was made worse by the loudness of the chanting, so when I popped out of the metro, I found a chemist and treated myself to some over the counter pain relief. Then I was home and I peeled off my clothes, slipped into my own bed and fell asleep.

When I woke up, there were more group messages and text messages. By all accounts, the Cup was still doing the rounds accompanied by more drinking and presumably debauchery. Never let it be said that ice hockey players can't drink!

I knew that other teams would have had their exit interviews and sent their players home for the offseason by now. I was confused as to the timetable for how things would proceed from here. The exit interviews were the chance for the coaching staff to tell you what you needed to work on in the offseason and were an opportunity to put a bow on the season as a whole. They were also a chance to load up on free sticks and gear for the offseason and the chance to say goodbye to the staff for the year. I'm not sure what the back-office staff did in the offseason but I did know it was traditional to tip the equipment guys. They couldn't possibly not be paid for the summer, could they? I flicked a couple of the vets a text message in the next few days to figure out how much was an appropriate amount to tip them and was surprised to find out it was a solid five figures. But I guess that made sense. If there were twenty something players on the roster and they each gave $10k, then that would make $200k. If there were three or four equipment guys, that would make $50k each. Apparently some players would gift Rolexes or cars which would be a bigger amount but I didn't know if that would cause a tax issue. I guess an accountant might know. The last thing you'd want is a free brand-new car plus a visit from the IRS and a tax bill for the tax due on that income. I knew I was going to be in the big numbers next year and we'd just won the Cup, so I dropped an email to my bank manager and told him that I would need a good chunk of cash in the next week or two. Maybe $25-30k.

While I was logged into my account, I noticed that the league didn't muck around and there was a nice chunk of change in there

The Forty Year Old Rookie

as payment for winning the Cup - $250k plus change. The league gave the winning team a chunk of money – it was $6.5M in 2024. It was up to the team how they split it amongst the squad. So there was a nice deposit in the account looking back at me. Maybe the equipment guys could get $50k. They had really done a good job with the suit. I hadn't had to repair it at all, and the security of the whole equipment team looking after it and it being treated as nothing special, meant I could have relaxed for the whole season. I could have, but I hadn't of course. I had learned to relax by the end of the season but for the beginning of the season from the preseason games all the way through to the first five or six games of the regular season I had been incredibly tense the whole time, worried about whether someone would find my secret or steal the suit.

The end of the year would consist of the Cup Parade through the city, the exit interviews and then, sometime in the summer, there would be a single day where you could have the Cup for the whole day. Players typically took the Cup to their hometowns, whether that was in their home countries back in Europe or into the small country towns where they were brought up. The Cup would be accompanied by the same two handlers with dark suits and white gloves who would protect it as best they could from the more dangerous shenanigans that players would submit the Cup to.

C. G. Lambert

The Cup had been used as a baptism font, been eaten out of, drunk from, pissed into, vomited into, used as a serving dish and those were the tamer usages.

Before social media, I was sure there were some even edgier uses. Hence the need for two full time minders. But I'm sure their backs would be turned at some point.

I would need to think of what I would like to do with the Cup on my day with it. I had cut off my past prior to the Training Camp, so I wouldn't be revisiting where I played my beer league games. I could take it to the fire station and police stations that the team had adopted.

Maybe swing past the hospitals that I had visited. I could take it to any and all of the beer league rinks and the players there would appreciate seeing it. There wouldn't be any shortage of people who'd love to see it.

***

And that was the story of my first season as a professional ice hockey player. For those keeping score at home, I made a lot of money. My hockey-related income alone was something like this:

$775,000 Base Salary
$1,500,000 Performance Bonuses
$2,250,000 Total Contract Income
$1,000,000 Winning skills competition at the All-Star Game
      $0 Losing All-Star Game (it goes to charity anyway)
$250,000 Winning the Stanley Cup
$20,000 Winning the Presidents' Trophy
$1,270,000 Additional Income

$3,520,000 Total Income

My agent took 5% of the contract and didn't commission the All-Star Game Competition money but did commission the Stanley Cup and Presidents' Trophy bonuses.

I paid the extra to get them to handle all of the taxes because you pay taxes in every city you play in. Who wants to do all the tax paperwork in 30 plus different jurisdictions?

Agent's fees: $2,520,000 @ 5% = $126,000

Taxes for players range from 52.3% (Montreal: the highest tax jurisdiction) all the way down to 35.78% (6 different US markets), depending on the amount received.

	Montreal	Typical	Lowest
Income	$3,520,000	$3,520,000	$3,520,000
Agent	$126,000	$126,000	$126,000
Taxes	$1,841,000	$1,732,546	$1,259,420
Net	$1,553,000	$1,661,454	$2,134,580

So leaving aside the chances of each team winning the Stanley Cup, if you chose where to play purely on the tax rate, it could be worth $581,580 more and that's on an entry level contract. On a $15M contract, the difference comes closer to $2.5M.

Looking at my healthy bank balance, I knew that I would probably spend some time in the next few weeks looking for a place to buy nearby. Or maybe something halfway between the training facility and Alex's place.

Maybe I would purchase some gym gear because I would be expected to turn up for Training Camp in good condition. I thought of my efforts off the ice in my first Training Camp and smiled wryly. I might need a personal trainer. There might just be the expectation of an improvement there. Maybe I'd even try a few games without the suit. Maybe.

The End

Acknowledgements

I know how to do two things: play ice hockey badly and write books good. The words in this book were made better by my editors, Gwyn Kipling and Angela Pearse.

I was helped no end by the agents who agreed to sit down and chat about the business. I need to give heartfelt thanks for the time and expertise of Rick Curran, Sean Coffey, Jason Harshaw, Mark Toof and Darren Ferris. Any errors are mine and made despite their guidance!

To all the players I've played with and against over the years, many thanks for the competition, for the yarns and for the beers after the games. I can't list you all, but a special thanks to Alex Spiers, Ben Mitchell, Dean Fotti, Gavin "Duds" Hall, Peter Rooke, and especially Matthew Chan. Thanks to Debbie Rooke and Wendy Hall for being the best bench bosses.

Thanks Ange for the awesome cover art.

Books by C.G. Lambert

UNCLE REGGIE SERIES (Geek Lit)

The Girl From Wonderland

The Man In The Hotel Ceiling

The Kids Who Lived In A Hole

OTHER

The 40 Year Old Rookie (Sports)

You Had Me at Ice Cream (RomCom)

The Illiterate Prince (Fantasy)

NON-FICTION

Adventures in Analytics (Non-fiction)

About the Author

C.G. Lambert was born the second of seven children and raised in South Auckland, New Zealand. His pre-writing career consisted of applying for whatever job sounded interesting, leading to time as an International Banker, a Music Manager, Web Developer and Analytics Manager. He loves travel (you can read about it at etrip.tips), holds dual citizenship (NZ/UK), a Bachelor of Arts and an MBA. He currently resides in the UNESCO City of Literature, Edinburgh with his partner.

www.ingramcontent.com/pod-product-compliance
Lightning Source LLC
Chambersburg PA
CBHW011126070526
44584CB00028B/3796